Frances I Kershaw

Baby

A study of baby life

Frances I Kershaw

Baby

A study of baby life

ISBN/EAN: 9783741183157

Manufactured in Europe, USA, Canada, Australia, Japa

Cover: Foto ©Lupo / pixelio.de

Manufactured and distributed by brebook publishing software (www.brebook.com)

Frances I Kershaw

Baby

BABY:

A

STUDY OF BABY LIFE.

BY

FRANCES I. M. KERSHAW,

AUTHOR OF

"BOBBIE AND BIRDIE,"

"THE GAMEKEEPER'S LITTLE SON," &c.

LONDON:
BURNS AND OATES, GRANVILLE MANSIONS,
ORCHARD STREET, W.

This true study of Baby-life and thought is lovingly dedicated by the author to all the Babies of St. Wilfred's Parish, York.

Feast of the Annunciation,
　March 25, 1883.

INDEX.

I.	Guess-Work	1
II.	A Christmas Box	13
III.	Baby Life	24
IV.	Nob'dy Ense	35
V.	Baby's Expedition	55
VI.	Master Me	85
VII.	Bears	110
VIII.	The Nun's Cross	124
IX.	Christmas Again	140
X.	Finishing Touches	160

BABY.

CHAPTER I.

GUESS WORK.

"A big little family," mother calls hers, I don't mean my mother, I who am telling the story. She is no relation, only it comes natural to call her so, you know, because mothers are mothers and nothing less all the world over. *This* mother besides is so especially a mother. She has more chicks under her wing than even the old hen in the orchard coop, who brought out of their shells eight downy balls the other day. I don't say that mother's chicks are so obedient though. She may cluck to them a great many times, and they pay no heed; whilst the old hen has only to chuckle to herself in a quiet way over her meal, and immediately all her family are flapping and fluttering to get under her wing, with the far-fetched notion in their heads that a hawk must be somewhere about.

Let me see—how many are there of them!—the children I mean, not the chicks. It almost cracks one's brain to reckon up!

As for remembering *ages*, I have given that up long ago.

I used to remember their *number* by the days of the week once upon a time, but there are more children than days now. There are nine of them, I think; but I can't be sure. I may be forgiven, however, if I miss a few out, like the Irishman who could'nt count all his master's pigs, because one was running about!

They are always running about—these children! I am sure the secret of perpetual motion lies snugly hidden amongst them somewhere.

One really expects to find a few legs that have run themselves off left about the house and garden. But somehow they never are!

Of course you want to hear the children's names before we get on any further. Children always do. I used to wonder whether Shakespeare could ever have been a child, to say such a thing as "What's in a name." Dear me, there is an immense amount! Don't we know at once what sort of people Sarah, and Betsy, and Sam are; and what sort of people Adelaide, Laura, and Claude are by their names, even without having the pleasure of knowing their little selves?

Well, the names of this pack of children are—first and foremost—Osyth; dear, good, womanly old Osyth—a little mother in herself, and somewhere about fourteen years of age.

After Osyth, they go down hill step by step—about a year between each; so you must calculate how old the rest are, if you want to know: it would try my patience too much to tell you.

Next comes Magdalen—Moonie, as she is generally called; because she is so often far away in her thoughts, building air-castles; even when she is sitting beside you, and you are trying to put such common-place things as grammar and arithmetic into her.

Then comes a triangle of boys—Cuthbert, a big, honest, bragging school-boy; with a large layer of good stuff in his composition, underneath another layer of grumpy-growlishness (I can't find a better word for it); so that you have to rake up the one to get at the other very often. And I think his mother knows most about *that*.

Then comes Aloysius, who is just *a boy*—devoted to "grub" and slang.

Caryl is a merry grig, who is always either just getting into a scrape, or just getting out of one. It never troubles him much which of the two it is. Caryl is one of those happy, light-hearted people, who seem to live in the air and on love, and trample carelessly on the things that would make other folks miserable.

Then there are the twinnies, Kenneth and Edith—quiet, sickly little people, who cling very much to one another, and have all their smiles, and tears, and sicknesses in common, to everybody's amusement.

Next comes the pickle of the family, Bruno— a roguish, curly-pated piece of goods, aged eight; and last of all—Daisy, the pretty, rosy, dolly-dumpling of a girl, whom they call baby, for want of a better attempt at one.

I don't think I need introduce you to the children's mother. You must get to know her for yourselves. For it is harder to say what a mother is than anything else; unless it is to say what she is not. Like the old rhyme, you must take it for granted that she is " Sugar and spice, and all that's nice!"

As for mother's face, it is the holiest I know. You can see all her children in it, and a great deal more, framed in a glory of patient love and loving patience.

The childrens' father we shall not have much to do with just now. He is an officer, away in India. But he sends very long, loving letters to his children by every mail, full of kisses, and hopes that when he sees them again, he may find them "better than best." Father expects a great deal of his bairns. Eh, and he *is* proud of them!

Now let me introduce you to the family group.

Lessons for to-day are over, aud everybody feels a little bit dull and dreary this November time. There is a sort of fog in the school-room as well as outside.

Cuthbert gives the fire a vicious poke to cheer it up; and the rest of the children—except the twinnies, who prefer to keep each other company at the table,—squat before it on the rug.

No one says anything for some time.

By and bye the silence becomes too much for Master Caryl. He gives a sharp whistle which startles everybody, and then remarks—

"Can't anybody speak? Daisy, have you 'lost your little tongue,' as Nanna says?"

"If you want people *not* to talk, the best way to do it is to ask them to!" says Cuthbert solemnly.

Magdalen comes down from the moon.

"When nobody talks for a long time, it's the angels coming amongst us," she says. "Osyth, what about Christmas? I suppose you'll have everything to settle this year with Miss Norton. What are we going to have? And who will be the angel to bring us our presents?"

"Its so long beforehand to ask such questions, Mag.," says Osyth. "Father has'nt said anything about what he is going to send yet. Something good it's sure to be! November is'nt done, and there's a large piece of December to go before Christmas. I suppose we shall have to manage things ourselves as mamma is'nt well enough to help us; and Daisy will make a dear little angel, as Edith did last year."

"Why we had *two* angels last year, Osyth,"

interrupts Bruno. "Don't you remember how odd it was? Edie would'nt be an angel unless Kennie was one too. So we had to have an extra angel. How we all laughed to be sure! Father was here then. Poor father! How he'll be thinking about us all this Christmas!"

"I think it's awfully jolly to begin to talk about Christmas now," says Aloysius. "It's next best to having it. Let's all say what we'd each like to have for our biggest present. Of course we shall have a lot—more than we can carry! But we'll each say what father's and mother's is to be."

"We'll roast some chesnuts then," says Cuthbert; "and whoever's nut cracks first, shall say what he'd like to have."

Osyth brings out the bag of nuts, and a whole row of bright little brown things are soon safely on the bar.

The children watch them as if all their future depended upon them.

"Crack! Fiz-z!"

"That's your's, Moonie!" cries Bruno, clapping his hands; "lucky you! What'll you have? Out with it!"

"A thinking-cap and a blue moon," suggests Cuthbert gravely.

"How unkind of you, Cuthie!" says Magdalen laughing good-naturedly;

"No, I should like,—I should like"—

"Quick!" cries Bruno again. "Osyth's chesnut is just going!"

"Crack! Fiz-z!"

"Hurrah for old Osyth! Now, Moonie!"

"It is'nt much use wishing," says Magdalen; "but I should like—yes! a new fairy-tale book —with not all old stories."

"Now Osyth" says Cuthbert, "something sensible for you, no doubt;—a frying-pan, or a pair of winter stockings!"

Osyth laughs.

"I know what I wish," she says.

"Well?" says Caryl impatiently.

"I wish that mother may get better very soon, and be able to spend Christmas with us, after all."

"Osyth, you're just like 'Beauty and the Beast,'" says Magdalen.

"Take care that your 'red rose' does'nt do arm like hers! Do'nt you want anything else?"

"I should'nt *mind* a nice new work-box, well fitted up," says Osyth, modestly.

"Crack! Fizz."

"It's the twinnies'," says Cuthbert. "Of course, their nuts go off together. I never met with such children!"

"We did'nt put any nuts to roast!" complain both twins at once.

"But I put them for you. What do you wish? Both the same thing, I suppose! It's well you two never quarrel!"

The twins blush, and they then actually do say what they wish, and together :—

"A baby."

"Nonsense," says Caryl; "wish for something that you can have."

"Mother could buy one," says Daisy. "I should like a baby too."

"I guess they'd cost a lot," remarks Bruno.

"Well, don't all go wishing for babies," says Cuthbert, "one would be all very well, but to have a houseful of them would be too much of a good thing."

"Daisy's our baby," says Osyth, fondling the little girl by her side.

"I'm not going to be a baby any more," that young lady asserts sturdily; shaking her curly head out of Osyth's hands, "mother says I'm growing quite big. I don't have my high chair at table now, and I learn lessons like the rest of you."

"Crack! Fizz!"

"All right, Daisy. We won't call you baby then. Wish! that's your nut," says kind Osyth.

"A baby," says Daisy; "and a nice cradle lined with pink for it, and let me rock it!"

"Crack! Fizz!"

"There, Caryl—what a beauty! That's your's. Wish on, old fellow!" says Cuth.

"I'll back Daisy," says Caryl; "I'd like to have another youngster squalling in the house, they're good fun."

"Crack!"

"What a mean nut, Aloysius! What do you want?" says Caryl.

"Well, I shall have to go in for the baby like the rest, I suppose," says Aloysius, with his mouth full of chesnut; "And I should like an extra lot of good things to eat."

"Crack!"

"You *do* like eating, Al.!" says Bruno. "Now my wish! A baby for a Christmas-box like the rest, and father home to have jolly larks with us!"

"You'll not get either, it's my humble opinion, dear man!" says Cuthbert; "however, there's no harm in wishing. You may sigh for the moon, if you like."

"I should'nt like," says Bruno; "'cos Moonie'd be in it."

"Where would Miss Magdalen be?" inquires a voice at the door, and old Nanna, the nurse, pokes her head in.

"In the moon, Nanna, Bruno said!" says Daisy, Nanna's great pet.

"I won't have my Miss Maggie aboozed," says Nanna, joining the group before the fire. "Bless me, chesnuts! What are you all doing?"

"O we're having ever such fun!" says Daisy, clapping her hands; "We're thinking about what we'd like for our big present at Christmas. And nearly all of us want a baby."

"Bless the children!" cries old Nanna; "One a-piece! And where would all the cradles come from?"

"Oh, no, Nanna; only one," say the twins. "It would be so nice to play with. *We* settled we'd like it first."

"And what is it to be—a boy or a girl?" asks Nanna.

"O, we had'nt thought about that," says Magdalen; adding with grand impartiality;—"I suppose boys are always nicest."

"And what'll you give me if I buy you one?" asks Nanna.

"Half our good things at Christmas," the twins volunteer.

"I think I'll wait till it comes, and then see," says Aloysius sagely.

"Will you get us one, really and truly?" asks Daisy incredulously.

"Bless your little heart, I'll do my best!" says Nanna. "When is it to be?"

"On Christmas day!" shout all the young ones; "A Christmas-box, you know, Nanna!"

Nanna nods her head very sagely, and departs.

"Will she really do it?" the children ask each other breathlessly, as the door closes on her.

And some say yes, and some say no.

But it is only guess-work, after all!

CHAPTER II.

A CHRISTMAS BOX.

THERE is a beginning to everything, you know—sometimes bad, and sometimes good, but always a beginning.

There was a beginning to you. I daresay you don't remember it, so you will have to take it on faith.

And there is a beginning to the joys and fun of Christmas-tide.

Of course the *real* beginning was hundreds of years ago, in a little royal town called Bethlehem. Christmas began in a stable, among the cows and horses; and its joy was, on earth at least, pretty much shut up for some time in two most loving hearts—that of the Mother Mary and of Holy Joseph. And it was all about a little Baby—their Christmas gift!—The little God-Baby who was born that day, and laid in the manger; and who has made all our Christmas days bright and gay and happy ever since.

But this Christmas day has another beginning besides this for the little Mayhews. I am not going to tell you what it is just yet, but only to stir up your curiosity, so that you may want to know all in good time!

Snow is on the ground; snow on the great black elms and oaks; snow on the roofs of the houses; snow coming gently down from the cushiony white clouds like eiderdown everywhere. It is a real Christmas-tide, indoors and out!

The house is dressed in greenery and crimson berries from "top to toe." The great log-fire blazes, and spits, and crackles with all its might in the big hall.

Cuthbert, Aloysius, and Caryl, have rolled the yule-log in between them, and mounted it on its fiery throne, much to Bruno and Daisy's delight.

"It's a famous Christmas day, this," says Caryl; "outside and in! I wonder when the presents are coming?"

"Are we going to have them here?" says Daisy.

"No, in the schoolroom, of course," says Aloysius, rubbing his hands. "I expect they'll be calling for you to make you an angel soon, Daisy!"

"What's Osyth doing?" asks Cuth.

"Ever so busy in the schoolroom with Miss Norton. The door is locked, so depend upon it they're up to something," says Caryl.

"I peeped through the keyhole, but I could'nt see anything but a shine of blue, and pink, and all sorts of colours, and I heard ever such a lot of paper rattling."

"Hurrah!" from all the youngsters. "Then its *beginning*."

And so it is.

Just then Osyth's serious face pokes itself in at the door mysteriously.

"Daisy?" say all the children in a breath.

Osyth nods, and disappears with Daisy in tow.

For some seconds after this the children nod smilingly at one another, until they look quite a nodding party; and then they laugh outright at the funniness of so much nodding.

"We're every bit like a lot of red poppies in a field!" says Magdalen.

"Except that we are'nt red, and we're not growing in a field," says sober Cuthbert.

"People say that other peoples' eyes are like the blue sky in poetry," argues Magdalen.

"And they're about as much like it as your's are like the moon, Moonie!" retorts Cuthbert.

"Don't get squabbling on Christmas-day, please," says Caryl; so good-naturedly that no one minds, but everybody heeds. "Mother says that when people have really blue eyes they are always mad."

"And horses are blind when they have blue eyes" says Aloysius.

"Don't you know the butcher's Jenny has one blind eye?"

"Hush!" says Bruno; "there's something coming."

"Some *one*, you mean," says Aloysius; as Osyth opens the door.

"Everything's ready," she says; "And Miss Norton says you're all to come."

"Hurrah!" cry all the children in a breath; and out they tumble, higgledy, piggledy, into the schoolroom—except the twins, who always walk together in very orderly fashion.

"Whoo-o-o!"

Say all the children under their breath.

The schoolroom—dingy place!—is got up like a fairy palace—all coloured tapers, gold and silver stars, and wreaths of leaves and flowers. The long rows of dreary old lesson-books are hidden by a splendid crimson curtain, which trembles slightly, as though something more lively than books were behind it.

"Take your seats, please, chicks," says Miss Norton, the children's governess.

There is a long sort of divan by way of a seat.

"Where's the angel?" whispers Bruno.

But before anyone can say so much as "Jack Robinson" in answer, even if they wish too, out pops Daisy from behind the crimson curtain.

She is'nt a bit Daisy's own little self. She wears a long white gauze dress, with golden stars down the front, and a wreath of hot-house flowers on her own golden curls. Gold wings are most ingeniously fastened to her shoulders, so that she can flap them beautifully by just moving her arms.

Caryl give a short, quick whistle of pleasure, after his fashion, and the Daisy-angel flaps herself up to the twins, and gives them a chessboard, a present from father. The chessmen are all in most delicate Indian carving.

Then comes something for Cuthbert, and for all the children by turns; and again and again, until poor Daisy's arms are quite tired, and the children can hardly hold their heap of treasures safely.

"It's not at all nice to be an angel," says Daisy; "I do pity them! You can't imagine how much one's wings get in one's way."

"I expect we should get used to them in time," says Moonie. "I've often thought I should like to fly. I *do* in my dreams sometimes!"

"Now we've got everything, I suppose," says Cuthbert. "How good everybody is to us! I declare I've got the very racquet I wanted, and the new cage for my Polly."

"You haven't got everything yet," says old Nanna. "I've got the very best in store for you. What'll you give to see it?"

"Nanna's kept her promise!" cry the younger children.

"Nanna's borrowed a baby to make fun!" cry the elder ones.

"Nanna's got an enormous doll for Daisy!" says Cuthbert.

But Nanna only nods her head wisely, and says—

"Come and see!"

"Come where?"

"Into mother's room."

"It's sure to be something good and real," says Cuthbert, "if it has to do with mother. Mother never lets a fellow be cheated. Come along!"

So the party file off to their mother's room, more quietly this time; for they are very thoughtful people, and mother is never strong enough to bear much noise at the best of times. When she is worse than usual, the children try to "suppress" themselves just a little, like Alice in Wonderland's Guinea-pigs.

Mother's curtains are drawn, the blinds are down, and the room is almost dark.

"Well?" say the children, a trifle impatiently.

Nanna lights the lamp, and takes the children one by one to see mother. Mother does'nt say anything. She kisses them, and looks very happy. Then she just opens the corner of a blanket bundle close to her, and lets them peep in.

"Oh!" says Osyth, as she takes her peep.

She is going to say something more, but Nanna puts up her finger, and Osyth is silent.

The same happens when Magdalen and Cuthbert go up.

But Bruno cannot contain himself so well.

"What is it Nanna?" he says. "It's funny, and pink, and warm."

"Hush, Master Bruno!" says Nanna. "Now, Miss Daisy, dear!"

"Why," says Daisy, as she is lifted up; "I declare—I do declare—it's a real baby!"

"A real baby!" echoes Bruno. "Are they like that when they are little?"

"Nanna's kept her word," says Magdalen.

"Are we going to keep it, Nanna?" the twins ask in a breath.

"That's as your mother pleases," says Nanna; her face all a-twinkling with smiles.

Mother does'nt say anything, but she hugs the little bundle closer to her.

"Mother's not for giving it up," says Cuthbert; "so I suppose it's settled, and we keep it for good."

"It's grand," says Caryl; "ever so much

better than any other live thing we've got. I'm sick of birds, and dogs, and cats."

"Mind you don't teach it to fight and use slangy words, Master Caryl!" says Nanna, shaking her fist at him.

"He ain't old enough," says Aloysius. "I guess he can't do much more than eat yet, can he? It must be jolly to have nothing else to do all day but eat!"

"Oh! oh! Al.!" says Daisy, opening her eyes wide; "you *are* greedy!"

"May I hold the dear little thing just a minute, Nanna?" begs Osyth. "I'll be very careful, and sit on this low chair!"

So Nanna gives the warm blanket bundle into Osyth's motherly arms.

Hereupon, of course, there is a grand chorus of:—"Oh, do let me hold it,—the dear, sweet, toottle-um baby!"

"And I have'nt had it yet!"

With warnings from those who *have* had their turn.

"Be careful!"

"Don't let it drop!"

"You'll break it!"

As if the new baby were some grand exhibition doll.

So they all have their turn; Cuthbert last.

He is rather shy of baby—the big fellow! There is so little of it! He must hold it though, or the others will laugh, and it might hurt his mother's feelings. She is evidently very proud of her baby, small as it is.

Cuthbert gets a good grip of the blankets with both hands, and holds the baby very steadily for a moment. But he does'nt feel by any means comfortable with it.

"Wah-h-h! Squeak!"

"Nurse! Nanna!" cries poor Cuthbert in great alarm, offering baby wildly to whoever will take it off his hands; "I don't know what's happening to it. It's yelling horribly!"

And Nanna gives baby back to its mother, laughing heartily at the boy's dismay.

"You'll have to learn to put up with plenty of that before you've done," she says, by way of comfort. "You should have considered such drawbacks before you asked for a baby, Master Cuthbert!"

"I did'nt bargain for the yelling," says Cuthbert grimly.

"You used to 'yell' once, sir!" says Nanna, hot in the baby's defence.

"I won't have it aboozed, b'ess it' little heart!"

"What's its name?" asks Daisy.

"It has'nt got one yet," says Nanna. "Suppose you all find a nice one for it. There are so many of you with three names a-piece, that it'll be hard to find a new one for this baby—bless it!"

"Call it Christmas, as it's born on Christmas-day," suggests Caryl.

"Call it Plum-pudding!" says Aloysius. "That would be a new name, and always make one think of something good, even when Baby is bad."

"Eating again, Al.!" snubs Daisy.

"I should like to know who lives without eating!" retorts Aloysius; "Not you, Daisy!"

"Call it Noel," say the twinnies. They have just begun to learn French, and are very proud of their knowledge.

"Mother's nodding," says Magdalen; "That's going to be the name. How clever of the twins to think of it!"

And Noel is the name of the little Mayhew's biggest present—their Christmas-box.

"Won't father be glad?" says Osyth. "Who'll write and tell him first?"

"I will," says Magdalen.

"I'll put a bit of a postscript to your letter then," says Caryl.

CHAPTER III.

BABY LIFE.

I DON'T mean to make this a regular stiff, out-and-out story; so don't expect it, or you will be disappointed. I am going to give you little pictures of my Baby's life.

It began with not much more than eating, sleeping, and a little crying—not very much! Noel was very like other babies in every way, I think, for the first short stage of his life. He was'nt a model baby by any means, for he lived to grow up. He was'nt born with a silver spoon in his mouth either, so far as I know.

People said all kinds of things about him; what he was, and what he was'nt, and what he was going to be. But he was a very calm, peaceable Baby, with a will of his own, so he just took his own way quietly in spite of all of them.

Old Betty White, the washerwoman, came in on purpose to see the Baby one day, and to tell her cronies what she thought of him.

Baby was asleep, and would'nt wake to look at her and be admired. So Betty went away saying he had beautiful eyes—just the only part of him she had'nt been able to see!

Other people gave it as their opinion that he would turn out a dreadful child to manage, with a will of his own as stiff as a poker;—the last of a family always was more trouble than all the rest put together.

"*You* may say what you please," says Nanna loftily to these old croakers; "It won't alter my mind a scrap. I don't believe in your children that hav'nt no wills, and bend about like barley in the wind. He's a beautiful boy as ever was. I never had such another to do for. And he'll be as beautiful inside as out! I consider him every bit the flower of the flock, dear lamb!—Not but what they're every one of 'em flowers, bless' em!"

And everyone knows there's no contradicting Nanna about her children. She won't hear a word said against them.

"I say, Nanna," says Bruno one day, "Baby's a long time getting big. When will he be able to have larks with Daisy and me? I'm tired of seeing him so small!"

Well, if that's not downright impudence!" says Nanna. "You never grew one half so fast yourself as does this dear Baby, bless it!"

"I wonder why Babies don't *begin* big," says Magdalen slowly, on her way to the moon.

"'Cos they would'nt fit into their cradles, I s'pose," says Daisy. "And then—fancy having to carry a grown-up baby!"

"But perhaps they could walk by themselves," suggests Bruno.

"Then they would'nt be Babies," says Daisy; "'cos Babies *can't* walk. So there!"

"*I* know what Daisy's doing, Nanna!" says Bruno, to turn the conversation. "She's making—"

"O Bruno, it's a secret! *Don't* tell," implores Daisy; tears coming into her big blue eyes.

"Why should'nt people tell secrets, Daisy?" says Bruno teazingly; "Besides, mother says she ought to know everything!"

"But if you tell Nanna, she'll tell Baby, and then, *of course*, it'll be of no use. I'll give it all every bit up if you do," says Daisy dolefully.

"Master Bruno, I do believe you get a bigger teaze every day," says Nanna, coming to the rescue; "I'm sure it's very good of Miss Daisy to be friends with you when you are so unkind to her!"

"Daisy likes me all the better when I teaze her well; don't you, Day?" says Bruno coaxingly. "You would'nt care a scrap about a brother that did'nt teaze, would you, Daisy?"

"N-no; I don't—think—I should;—at least not *always*," Daisy admits dubiously; "But you won't tell, will you, Bruno?"

"About the shoes?—no, not a syllable!" says Bruno decidedly. "I never mean't to. I only wanted to put you in a wax."

"Oh, Bruno!"

"It really is too bad, Master Bruno!" says Nanna.

But the secret comes out at last of its own accord.

Nanna finds a tidy parcel laid at the foot of Baby's cot, wrapped in an unmistakeable page from Daisy's round-hand copy-book.

Inside it is a pair of tiny baby-shoes, knitted in odds and ends of wool of divers colours, with many stitches dropped, and telling tales of the not over-clean fingers that made them.

Nanna smiles to herself, and whispers—"Bless the little dear! What pains she have taken, to be sure!"

Presently Daisy's head peeps in at the door.

"Did you find anything anywhere, Nanna?" she asks, innocently.

"Well, I did find a most beautiful present for Baby in his cradle," says Nanna; "and I really believe it was a pair of little woollen shoes!"

"And who do you guess made them, Nanna? Won't you put them on him now? I do want to see his little pink toes! Stay a moment though, and I'll call all of them."

Presently the Mayhew tribe bounce in. Fortunately Baby is awake, and crowing in his cradle.

Nanna puts on her thinking-cap for a moment,

Baby Life. 29

then she takes up Baby, and uncovers the aforesaid pink toes. Next follows a kissing process all round. It is the greatest honour to be allowed to kiss Baby's toes. Even big Cuth does'nt consider it beneath him to put his lips to those dear little wax-like feet, though he blushes very much over it.

"Poor old Cuth! He's just as red as a beet after kissing Baby," remarks Caryl. "He don't half like kissing—now I just do!" At which speech poor Cuthbert grows more beet-like than ever.

"I do believe the shoes are too little," says Daisy, sorrowfully, as she tries to put them on with Nanna's help.

"Why you've left no way to get into them, Daisy dear," says Osyth.

"Oh, dear, dear! I quite forgot that," says Daisy; "but never mind,—they'd be too small anyhow."

"Could'nt Baby get in at the side where all the stitches are dropped?" suggest the twins.

"No," says Daisy mournfully, "I shall have to give it up. But you can't think what a lot of my playtime they took to make. I had to undo them ever so often, and the wools would get into a tangle."

"I'll show you how to make a really nice pair for Baby, Daisy," volunteers kind Osyth. "I have some white wool that will just do, and you shall tie them with blue ribbon."

"I say, its a sign that Baby's growing pretty fast though," says Bruno; "if he can't squeeze into Daisy's socks anyhow!"

But now I think it is time to tell you how this poor Christmas Baby nearly came to an untimely end.

The younger children are playing "Punch and Judy" in the nursery one day. Baby is crowing peacefully to himself on a rug. It is a fine afternoon, and the windows are all open. Suddenly the children stop short in their game. They have just discovered that it is "the play without Hamlet."

"Where's the Baby for Mr. Punch?" exclaims Daisy.

"O dear! O dear!" wails Bruno. "Nanna said her rags were beginning to smell,—she was so old and dirty; so I made a jolly bonfire of her."

"Then what shall we have instead?" questions Daisy dolefully. "There's nothing to have. Sarah Dulcibella is too smart, and my Evelyn Hildegarde has gone to the dressmaker's for a new gown—besides she's too small."

"*I* know," mischievous Caryl flings behind him as he leaves the room. "Try the Baby."

"Hurrah, the Baby!" echoes Bruno. "Happy thought! Nanna isn't here to say anything, and *he* won't mind. Will you, Baby?"

"Och, och, och! Guggle, uggle, goo-oo-o!" says Baby, staring at a light wandering over the ceiling.

"There! He says he'd enjoy it very much, doesn't he?" says Bruno.

"Anyway, it's quite as clear as the things Nanna believes he says about her," says truthful Daisy. "Let's have him then."

"I'll goggle, oggle, goo-oo!" says poor, luckless Baby, as Bruno seizes him.

"Not a *real* window!" plead the twins, as they see poor Baby lifted in mid air.

"Of course, goosies! What would be the good of a sham one?" retorts Bruno. "Now, Daisy, take him. Then when I have beaten you with the little wheelbarrow handle, give me the Baby, and I'll throw him out of the window."

"You won't beat hard?" stipulates Daisy.

"I'll only *pertend*," says Bruno. "You can tell me how it feels afterwards."

"And you won't let Baby *really* drop out of the window, Bruno?" This from the twns.

"Just as if I was likely to! I shall hold him tight in my teeth by his frock. I shall only *pertend* that too."

So the play goes on. Daisy receives her beating very submissively, and hands over the Baby to Bruno's tender mercies.

Fortunately, at this point the twins take alarm, and hurry off to warn Nanna that her youngest charge is in peril of his life.

"Kl-thick! goo-a-oo!" coos Baby sweetly, as he is hung out of the window by Bruno's teeth; while Daisy, who is a little bit nervous about the matter, has hold of his little pinafore behind.

Baby enjoys any out-of-the-way sort of position, and chuckles away to himself happily, quite unconscious, poor little man! that every moment may be his last.

"Now," says Daisy, "isn't it time to bring him in again?"

Bruno shakes his head.

"Do, Bruno!" begs Daisy. "Look, there are quite a crowd of people under the window, all staring up. I wonder what they want?"

A great crowd it is; but no one dare speak for fear of startling Bruno, and causing him to lose his hold of the unfortunate Baby.

Then comes Nanna into the nursery. She does not scream nor faint when she sees Baby's terrible danger. She does not rush at the boy, and try to drag Baby away. In just her quiet everyday voice, she says—

"Bring that Baby to me, master Bruno."

In comes Baby, still chuckling peacefully; and Bruno, red with his exertions, and more than proud of having been able to hold Baby so long by his teeth in mid air.

When Nanna gets her Baby again, she says nothing, does not even scold Bruno for his naughtiness. She hugs little Noel to her breast, and rocks him to and fro, crying quietly to herself.

"He did enjoy it so!" says Bruno.

"But you know it *does* seem a little dangerous," added Daisy, "of course, Clara Alicia never felt it when we let her drop out of window, poor thing! but then it might have hurt Baby!"

When Caryl comes in a quarter of an hour later, he finds Nanna still crying, with Baby in her arms.

"What's up, Nanna," he asks good humouredly, "what have those two been after."

"Hanging this precious Baby out of that window, master Caryl," answers Nanna, in awestruck tones, "only to think of that! Master Bruno, if ever I catch you at that game again, I'll, I'll,"—

But Nanna can get no further. She is not used to threatening her children, so she finishes up with a few more tears.

Caryl goes of with a long whistle, which says, —"A fellow will have to be more careful what he says before that mischievous Bruno again."

CHAPTER IV.

"NOBODY ENSE."

OF course in real life people only take one step at a time, and often find that too much for their nerves, but in story-telling nobody will scold us if we take a good many with a pair of those famous seven-leagued boots on. So I am going to skip over Baby's three first birthdays altogether, and set you down at that point where the young gentleman begins to chatter, and, as Caryl says, "to be interesting."

He is very fond of talking in his own little way, but I think still fonder of listening. People say so many things that are quite new to him. He had no notion that there were such wonderful things in the world. So he listens until his little mind becomes a storehouse of treasures, quite safe for the present, for Baby has no words to express all he knows. Some day it will come pouring out, and everybody will be astonished to find what a well-informed young man he is.

This morning we renew our acquaintance with

the Mayhew tribe in the nursery. They have one and all deserted the dingy school-room, and come upstairs for a glimpse of baby and of Nanna's mild, cake-suggestive face.

Baby is perched on the high window-seat, looking out into the busy street; Nanna beside him with her work, to prevent his falling down and breaking his crown, like Humpty Dumpty, of famous memory.

Magdalen is looking out too, in her own meditative way. To watch her eyes, you would think she saw nothing but clouds and air-castles, but she does manage to see much more than most people somehow.

"Nanna," she says presently; "there's that Barney Wheelan in the street—he's looking up at us. Oh, what a white face he has! He reminds me of—of—oh, yes! don't you know? the match-girl in my Andersen book! 'Melancholy,' would't you call him, Nanna? Is'nt he an orphan now?"

"Yes, my dear; him and his little sister, and she's a cripple, too, and deaf, and very sickly;" says Nanna, intent upon a gusset she is fitting on her work.

"What's *a norfer*, Nanna?" inquires baby, staring hard at the boy in question, to see wherein he differs from other boys.

"An orphan is some one who has neither Pa nor Ma, Master Noel, dear," says Nanna; "that's very sad, is'nt it?"

"Baby sink yit weddy sad," murmurs baby, with a sigh.

"Barney lives in the country, and he has'nt got anybody to love him," says Magdalen.

"Not got nob'dy ense—not got nob'dy to yove him!" echoes Baby half to himself.

"May I throw him out my sixpence, Nanna?" says Moonie. "Very likely he's had no breakfast. He looks as if he'd had nothing to eat for a month."

"Very well, my dear; if you wish," says Nanna.

So out goes Moonie's new sixpence from a very loving heart and hands, she sends it with such a good aim that it comes with a hard thump on to Barney's upturned nose. But Barney doesn't seem to pity his nose at all. He gives it a hard rub; and then grins with pleasure from one ear to the other, as he makes bows without end.

"Not got nob'dy ense!" echoes Baby once more when the window is shut, and Barney has gone off to turn his sixpence into something eatable. "I sink it's wenny sad to have nob'dy ense!"

"It's the dinner-party to-night in father's honour," says Moonie presently. "I don't think I'm glad. People do say such stupid things about the weather, and the country, and the servants, and their children. When I'm grown up, I won't give dinner-parties. I'll give beautiful balls on the lawn in the moonlight instead."

"Precious cold work they'd be!" remarks sober Cuthbert.

"Will Baby come downstairs to dessert, Nanna?" inquires Daisy.

"Of course he will, bless him!" says Nanna.

"'Torse he will," echoes Baby. "Baby have c'ean frock on, an' i' boo sash, an' 'e' wibbins on e' shoulder. Baby yike go down 'tar', 'cos it's 'i' berfday."

"Nonsense, Baby," says Daisy; "it's father's birthday. You had yours a long time ago."

"Baby have haif of ev'ybody's berfday," maintains Baby stoutly; "'cos Baby yikes e' berfday cakes an' e' desserts, and 'cos nob'dy ense wants a berfday."

"*I* want *my* birthday," says Daisy. "Don't you want yours, Bruno?"

Bruno nods. He can't afford words for an answer. He is busy spelling out a letter the postman has brought him this morning.

"Osif give Baby *her* berfday!" asserts Baby confidently.

"Yes, Baby shall have Osyth's birthdays," says Osyth kindly.

"*All* of dem?" inquires mercenary Baby.

"Yes, all of them."

"Den Baby vewy kind. He will take all of dem 'cos of de cakes. But Nanna says Baby gwow old soon, if he have many, many berfdays —old womin some day, Nanna says! Osif not grow old if se hav'int got no berfdays at all. Poor Baby! he's vewy good to Osif! Baby yikes 'e cakes an' 'e desserts."

Osyth laughs.

"I say, all of you," says Bruno from his letter, "here's news! Guess what it is."

"Aunt Bee's coming to-night, after all?"

"Not a bit of her! She's in Scotland."

"We're going down to dinner with the big folks!"

"Wish we were!"

"Cuthbert's going to Stonyhurst?"

"So he is; but you all knew that before. It's stale news."

"We are all going to the sea-side?"

"Don't make a fellow's mouth water, Caryl."

"Somebody's going to take us to the circus!"

"No, you'd never guess. It's not anything nearly so jolly. Me Stanley is coming for a week—'bless him!' as Nanna says. I'm sure I wish he'd stop away. He's such a perfect pig. He cares about nobody but himself. I expect we shall have a time of it with him. Baby, you'll have to entertain Me."

"Baby have a time wif him," echoes Baby. "'Es, Bu, Baby have a time wif him."

"What a parrot you are, Baby! Wouldn't Master Me be disgusted if we left Baby to entertain him!" says Bruno.

"Wif my toy sings," adds Baby.

"He is a proud young dog!" says Caryl.

"Don't be unkind. Perhaps he's grown better now," puts in Osyth.

"There was plenty of room for growing better anyway," says Bruno. "Well, he's coming; so we shall have to put up with him. Won't he spoil the remainder of our Midsummer holidays though!"

A general Mayhew groan.

"Spoil 'e Baby's holidays!" says Echo.

"It's all holidays for you," grunts Bruno. "Wait till your lessons begin, young man, and then see how you like them!"

"Yike 'em!" echoes Baby sweetly.

"Don't spend your day grumbling and growling," says Cuth sagely. "Mr. Marsden has promised to take us four big ones on to the rink at ten.

"And if it is'nt a quarter to ten now!" exclaimed Magdalen, looking at the clock; "and I have my buckle to find before I can go!"

"Look sharp about it then," says Cuthbert. "I'm off."

"Baby go on ye wink wif his buckons!" echoes Baby.

"Some day Baby shall go, and Osyth will show him how to skate," says Osyth, kissing the little man as she goes out.

"Car'l not kissed 'e Baby," complains Baby dolefully, when the party is gone, and only the twinnies and Bruno and Daisy left, "Car'l did forget 'e poor Baby."

"Grannie's coming to-night, Baby; is'nt that nice?" say the twins, coming to console Baby for Caryl's neglect. "She's coming to stay with us. You'll like Grannie ever so, Baby. She's got pockets perfectly *full* of lozenges, and such beautiful white curls!"

"Baby s'ant yike Grannie!" says Baby, turning sulky. He is very much hurt in his mind.

"You'll have to like Grannie, Baby," says Edie.

"Everybody does," adds Kennie.

"Baby id'nt ev'ybody!" says sulky two-year-old.

"She's got such pretty cheeks and caps, Baby," said Kennie coaxingly.

"And such a dear, sweet voice," adds Edie.

"Baby yike *ug'y* caps!" says obstinate Baby.

"He's cross," says Daisy; "leave him, and come and paint."

So the twins give up their task of comforting Baby in despair.

And Baby tucks his two fists into his eyes, and has a good howl over the unkindness of the world in general, and his corner of the world in particular.

"I wis' 'e night-time an' 'e party would come!" he sighs to himself by and bye, when his temper is mended.

And it does come at last.

Nanna, with a world of honest pride in her face, brushes up Baby's curly wig, puts on his softest white frock, and his bluest of blue ribbons, here, there, and everywhere.

"Now Baby must sit still till it's time to go down, and not mess his nice face," she says; setting him to the table with his favourite picture-book to look at.

"Baby no' yike c'ean flocks, 'cos he ca'nt mess 'em," says Baby presently; "an' 'e boo wibbins, an' 'e sash."

Nanna takes no notice of Baby. She is brushing Daisy's goldi locks.

"Baby yikes i' pink flocks," murmurs the young man at the table.

Then—"Paint-boxes is to paint wif. Baby hav'nt got no paper to paint wif!"

A pause. Then—"Paint-boxes is to paint flocks wif. Baby's vewy clevar!"

"Please to stand still, Miss Daisy," says Nanna; "If you don't want to have the brush in your eyes."

"'Tid'nt pink, it's boo," says Baby.

"Baby wanted a nice pink flock!"

Then—"It's nearny yike 'e wibbins," to himself.

"Baby is very quiet, Nanna," says Bruno. "Is he up to mischief, I wonder?"

"Bless the boy! he's good enough," says Nanna; "He's beginning to amuse himself nicely with his pictures now. He's not half nor a quarter the trouble you all was as babies."

"B'ess 'e boy!" echoes Baby softly; "He's not half 'e trouble, paintin'—amoosin' 'i'self nicey!"

"Nanna; oh, Nanna!" cries Daisy, whose hair is in apple-pie order, and who has come round to look at Baby; "He's *actually* got my paint-box, and he's made a perfect mess of his frock—it's all blue!"

"Boo flocks!" echoes Baby delighted, splashing the brush full of water and paint wildly down the front of his garment. "Baby's vewy clevar!"

"Dearie me!" exclaims Nanna, as she sees what ruin has been wrought to the clean white frock put on that very half-hour for the first time, "Baby, it is too bad—it really is!"

For once in her life dear old Nanna comes very near to scolding point. Baby takes it all very kindly and calmly. He is more than satisfied with himself.

"It's on'y boo," he says sweetly; "I wis' it had been pink!"

But he begins to cry when Nanna takes off the "boo flock," and brings another out of his drawer.

"Take away the paint-box, Miss Daisy," she says. "If it had'nt been there for him to have, he'd never have got it"—which is a fact not to be gainsayed.

"Is 'oo corse, Nanna?" inquires Baby; it is dawning upon him that matters are not quite straight with Nanna for some reason or other.

"Not with you, darling," Nanna can't help saying, as she kisses the innocent little culprit.

"An' I'se not corse wif 'oo, Nanna!" returns Baby sweetly.

At last mother's bell rings for the children to go down to dessert. Baby is posted at table between two old ladies who have taken a fancy to him. He cannot return the liking, but as he is a very polite Baby, he tries to make the best of a bad state of things.

The first old lady hands him a dish of raisins and almonds.

"May'nt have dem," says Baby; "dem makes 'e Baby ill."

"Then take some nice gingerbreads, my dear," suggests the old lady on Baby's other side.

"Baby don't yike them," says Baby, shaking his head.

Then come dishes crowding thick and fast round poor bewildered Baby; and at last, to everbody's surprise, up go two fists into Baby's eyes, and the old ladies, deaf though they are, catch the sound of a stifled sob.

"What's the matter little dear?" asks the old ladies in great alarm.

"What's the matter, Baby?" says mother, from the end of the table.

"It's 'cos of all dem 'gedder!" sobs Baby;

"all e' dishes is a-gedder, an' Baby *can't* eat awn of dem!"

"Don't cry, my dear; have anything you like!" says one old lady.

"But I'se *don'* yike," sobs Baby; "I'se on'y wants one of dem! I'se don' wan' to eat awn of dem!"

Mother sees what is the matter now. Poor Baby imagines that politeness will oblige him to take all that is set before him, and he feels overwhelmed.

"You need only take an orange if you like, Baby," she says.

And Baby clears up at once like an April day.

"Oran'sh is good!" he remarks. "Dey comes out of a summer countwy, Car'l says. Car'l knows all 'e books, an' all 'e lessins. Car'l yoves 'e Baby,—but Car'l wented out, an' Car'l forgot to kiss 'e Baby!"

The two old ladies don't understand Noel's baby-language, but they both smile down on him very benignly.

"Does peoples always laughs in 'e desserts?" inquires Baby at last. The old ladies smile on.

"I s'pose they does," Baby answers himself. "I sink it's vewy silly!"

"Does ev'ybody put on on'y half their flocks in 'e dessert?" says Baby again, when he has looked round the table. "Ev'ybody 'cept mover. I sink mover looks vewy pretty, wif e' gween woses an' i' ferns on her head!"

The old ladies smile on.

"I sink I'll get down," says Baby at last. He has tried in vain to start a conversation. "You'se don't yike talkin'—you'se yikes laughin'."

"Come here, Baby," says mother, when everybody has gone into the drawing-room—"Come and speak to grannie."

Baby sidles up to mother, with one finger in his mouth.

Grannie is sitting close to mother; she has even one of mother's hands in hers, which Baby does'nt half like—it seemed to imply a sense of possession; and what right has grannie to mother?

I just want to draw you a picture of grannie if I can. She has the mildest of grey eyes—a little dim, but beautifully loving and tender;

rosy cheeks, like the last apples of the year; a mouth that seems only made for sweet and gentle words—either to comfort unhappy people, or to make happy ones happier still. Her hair is snow-white, and tucked up into three little combs on both sides of her forehead. On her head she wears a soft white cap, that seems almost as if she must have been born in it—it is so much a part of her. You could not fancy the cap without grannie, or grannie without the cap. She wears always the same silky-dove-coloured dress, and that seems as if it had grown on her too. You never see grannie without her stick—a big bamboo, with a gold knob at the top and a character of its own—that her son brought all the way from India for her birthday thirty years ago.

She is the dearest old grannie you can imagine—from the crown of her head to the tip of her feet. Depend upon it, yours is nothing to her, or mine either. She seems made to be loved and to love. The touch of her hand carries a sort of comfort with it when you are in trouble. The glance of her eye helps you up and on when you are down-cast. She has a large silk "poppet," as she calls it, fastened to her waistband, and this poppet always holds a bountiful supply of goodies—chocolates, lozenges, and so forth—for any little folks who may happen to be near enough to eat them. It would be very hard to help loving grannie, but Baby means to try.

"What have you got to say to grannie, Baby!" asks mother, when Baby has been kissed, and is standing there silent and uncomfortable.

"Baby's not got nuffin' to say," returns Baby, hanging his head sheepishly.

"Not even to poor grannie, who has come such a long way to see him?" says grannie softy.

Baby is well-nigh conquered by that loving voice, but he feels he must hold his ground at any cost.

"Baby's not going to yove gwannie," he remarks, "'cos Baby did say so. But Baby's veddy soddy!"

"It was a very silly thing to say," Baby, says mother. "You'll have to forget all about it, and love grannie very, very much."

"Can't now, 'cos he said he wouldn't!" says Baby sorrowfully.

A funny little smile flies about grannie's sweet mouth, and she says to mother—"By and bye!"

"Tell grannie what you did to your nice clean frock, Baby," says mother. "Daisy's been telling me a shocking story!"

"Baby painted id boo," says Baby, a little ruefully. Everybody is so shocked at what he has done, though he can't see why. "Baby 'moosed hisself nicey."

"Poor Nanna!" says mother. "It was such a pity, Baby."

"'Esh," says Baby; but he doesn't see why. "Isn't flocks not to be painted?"

"No," says mother; and Baby sees why everybody is vexed with his clever work. But why shouldn't frocks be painted?

"You are very fond of painting, are you, Baby?" says grannie. "So was I when I was a little girl."

"A yitten girn!" echoes Baby in surprise.

"I did a very strange thing once. I took my paint-box into the garden, and painted all the white roses blue. But they didn't look nearly so nice in their new dress, so I took my little watering-can, and washed all the paint off again."

"Dat was nice!" says Baby, edging up closer to grannie.

"And I took to painting pictures afterwards, Baby; because I found that roses and frocks are best left their own colour. Will you paint me a picture, Baby?"

"Esh," says Baby. One of his little hands is in grannies now, keeping mother's company; but he is not thinking about that.

"Baby'll yove 'oo cap on 'oos nice face," he says presently, not to compromise himself.

"You may go and speak to Mr. Marsden now, Baby," says mother. "He is looking out for you."

"I'se don' yike 'peakin' to 'e peoples," says Baby; moving off slowly in the gentleman's direction.

Then—"Is'nt dere a nicer peoples wifout beards to 'peak to? I'se don' yike to be kissed wif 'e beards."

Baby's eyes light upon a tall, thin, æsthetically attired lady at the other end of the room. She has nobody to speak to her.

"I'se yike 'e yady yere," says Baby, toddling off to her straightway; "'cos nob'dy ense yikes her. 'Spec' she's a orphin!"

Baby squats down on the floor near to her.

"I sink oo's got nob'dy to talk to," he begins cordially. "Does 'oo yike talkin' or yarfin'?"

The lady starts as if a red-hot coal had fallen out of the fire dangerously near to her at Baby's voice, and then she draws her fadey velvet skirts carefully away from him.

"It's soft an' gway yike Smuts," poor Baby begins again. "'Muts is our pussen cat. Does 'oo yike pussen cats?"

"Yes, I am very fond of cats," says the lady nervously; "but I don't like babies, I never know what to say to them. You'd better go to somebody else. Look! Mr. Marsden wants you."

"I'se don' yike 'e peoples," echoes Baby. "I'se don' know what to say to yem. I'se yike 'oo, 'cos nob'dy ense yikes 'oo."

"How do you know that, Baby?" says the lady, a little bit tartly.

"'Cos peoples talks to peoples when yey yikes em," says Baby; "an' nob'dy talks to 'oo."

"You're a very philosophical baby," says the lady. "Do you know what that means?"

"It's a big say," says Baby; "I'se don' yike big says in 'e books. Has you got any babies?"

"No," says the lady—a little sharply this time.

"Havint you got nob'dy?" queries Baby again.

"No, nobody; I live quite alone."

"A orphin?" questions Baby, sadly and under his breath.

"Yes."

"Are'nt you beddy soddy?" pursues Baby with much sympathy.

"I should'nt mind a philosophical baby like you for a time. But they are not to be picked up every day."

"No?" says Baby doubtfully. He does not in the least understand what she means.

"Now you'd better go, child," says the lady presently. "You'll only be dull if you stay with me. I don't know how to talk to children."

"I'se don' want to talk," says Baby contentedly; "I'se sinkin."

"What are you thinking about—you bit of a thing?"

"I'se sinkin' lots o' sings," says Baby loftily. "I'se yike 'oo face."

"Why do you like my face?" asks the lady, feeling flattered at Baby's admiration. "It is'nt at all pretty like your mother's."

"I'se yikes 'oo face 'cos nob'dy ense does," says Baby gently.

"That's a very odd reason. How do you know they don't?"

"'Cos you's not got nob'dy," says Baby; "an' dere all lookin' at 'e udder ones. *I'se* yik 'oo!"

"I'm sure it's very kind of you," says the lady; "but I wish you would like someone else. Is'nt it nearly bed-time?"

"Baby don't go to bed till it's late, 'cos of 'e dessert, an' 'e white flocks," explains Baby.

Nothing will prevail on him to leave the lady of his choice. Until bedtime comes, he sticks to her side like a leech; and even when Nanna comes to carry him off tired and sleepy, his last glance is at the sharp-faced lady who has won his heart.

CHAPTER V.

BABY'S EXPEDITION.

"Baby, what a goose you were to stick to that pokery, cross, old dame last night," says Daisy next day. "Mr. Marsden was nodding to you to come over and over again. He told us a perfectly *sweet* story."

"I'se yike 'e yady," murmurs Baby shyly.

"No accounting for tastes!" says Caryl.

"Why do you like her, Baby?" says Bruno. "She's ugly and cross."

"'Cos nob'dy ense does," says Baby. "She's a orphin—she's not got nob'dy ense."

"Well, that's a queer reason! She looked as if she thought you a regular nuisance though. 'Tell you what—you'd better go and be her baby, I think, as she's got nobody else! Don't you think so, Caryl?"

Caryl nods. He is mending his cane, and has one end in his mouth, which prevents his speaking.

"Car'l says esh," says Baby softly. "Car'l always says 'e wight sings."

About a week after, a cool afternoon tempts the Mayhew family to go out of doors in different directions. Mr. Marsden calls for Cuthbert, Caryl, and Aloysius. Mama and grandmama have taken Osyth and Magdalen driving in the country. Daisy, Bruno, and the twins are with Miss Norton. Baby is being perambulated through the streets, shopping, with Kate the nurse-girl.

"S'ops is pwetty sings," says Baby; as Kate comes out of a draper's shop, and packs a parcel into the back of his pram. by way of a pillow. "I'se yike 'em. If Baby was 'e mans an' womins in 'e shop, he would always sit outside 'e door, an' yook in. 'Tid'nt pwetty in 'e inside."

"Baby yikes 'e moneys to buy 'e sings. Baby's got a shinin' shinnin' wot gwannie gaved him in his pockie to buy sussing."

Kate pays no heed to poor little chatterbox in the pram. She rumbles him on over the rough flags, and the noise of the wheels drowns his little bird-like treble. Her silly head is full of what people are thinking of her pretty face, and her nice new dress and hat. But Baby does'nt mind; he chatters on to himself.

"Baby sinks he will buy sussin' for Car'l, 'cos Car'l yoves 'e Baby. Baby sinks he will buy Car'l a weal, *weal*, big, kicken' pony wif his shinnin' wot gwannie gaved him. *Kin'* Baby, to give Car'l his nice noo shinin' shinnin'!"

The pram. comes to a stand-still.

"It's a woon-shop," says Baby. "Bernin-woon, he heard mover say Kate was to buy. Kate's got her fwen's in 'e woon-shop. Baby win have a wong time to wait. Poor Baby! He don' yike waitin' for Kate!"

"Now sit still, Master Baby," says Kate, coming out to look after her charge.

"It's a wenny yong time!" says Baby drearily. He is amusing himself by rubbing his clean little gloves over the dusty tire of the wheels, and watching the result with interest. The gloves are changing colour beautifully.

"Never mind!" says Kate, as she disappears again, "Kate'll buy him a cakie at the next confectioner's we come to!"

"Wif a yot of cuddants," adds Baby.

"Whose yat tumin' out of 'e woon-shop?"

A tall, sharp-featured lady it is, with a parcel in her hand.

She has a thin veil on, but clear-eyed Baby does not fail to recognise through it his friend of the evening party.

"I wis' s'e would yook at me!" he says to himself.

But the lady never once turns her eyes towards either perambulator or Baby. She goes straight on her way.

"Car'l said Baby'd better be 's yady's yitten boy," says Baby to himself.

"Car'l always says 'e wight sings. Mover's got awn of yem. Cuff, an' Moonie, an' Osif, an' Car'l, an' awn of yem. An' 'e yady's on'y got nob'dy. Baby win go, 'cos he's weddy soddy for 'e poor yady. Mover would tell 'e Baby to be kin'."

Baby scrambles out of his pram, in a second, and makes the best of his way after the lady, toddling along as fast as his two little feet will go. She walks at such a rate, that there is no catching her up.

On goes Baby. He will never give up a thing, once he had made up his mind to it.

"I wis' 'e yady would'nt yun so," he gasps presently; "Baby's not got any bref!"

"S'e's gettin' in a cab!" he exclaims at last.

"Ye horsen is takin' her away!"

And, standing still on the pavement by the long cab-stand, poor Baby watches his lady go off in the foremost cab with utter dismay.

"Have to go an' be her yitten boy 'nudder day!" he sighs, and turns to go back to pram. and Kate.

But this is impossible. In all his small life, Baby had never been here before; he does not know in the very least how he came. Besides, an excursion train has just come in at the same station near, and a crowd, armed with carpet bags and umbrellas, is pouring down the pavement. It will be upon him soon.

Poor, frightened Baby! He wheels about, and flies straight into the arms of the first cabby he meets. It happens to be a kind cabby with children of his own at home.

"Heyday! And what now, little man?" says cabby.

"He's *yost*!" says Baby, speaking dolefully in the third person. "He was tryin' to catch 'e yady wot got in 'e cab, an' she wented away. He's *yost*!"

And then comes something between sobs about "''e gwate cloud," "Kate," and "Bernin-woon."

"Was the lady your Ma!" asks cabby, putting himself between Baby and the crowd of jostling excursionists.

"No" says Baby; "he was only going to be her yitten boy, 'cos she's got nob'dy ense."

"Stepmother, I should guess!" says Baby's cabby to another. There are about half-a-dozen in a group round him now.

"A orphin!" says Baby, by way of explanation; "sh's not got nob'dy ense."

"It was Mrs. Doran," says one of the cabbies, "as took No. 144. I know where she lives. I've a single fare that-a-way, so I can take the child along."

"Esh," says Baby gratefully, and he puts his tiny paw into the big, rough palm held out to him.

Mounted beside cabby on the box, his tears still on his cheeks, Baby smiles and chatters away to his new friend.

"Cuff's goin' to Stonyhurst," he begins. "Is 'oo soddy!"

"Gee up, then! Hey? Is he though?"

"He's to have a big hamper of goodies to take with him," says Baby again. "Es 'oo glad!"

"Chuck, chuck! Get on wi' thee then, Lively!"

"She's called 'Lively,' is she?" says Baby, trying to hit upon some more congenial topic of conversation. "It's a pretty name."

"Gee-up, then! Yes, Lively's her name, to be sure."

"She does not 'gee-up,' as if she was lively," says Baby; watching the slow see-saw motion of the horse's four scare-crow legs with interest.

"Come, gee-up! Lively, old girl. She ain't so young as she was, little master; but she's very willin'."

"Yat's what mover had writed in 'e nouspaper to get a nursemaid when Kate goes!" remarks Baby. "Kate's got a 'young man,' do you know. I saw him one day in 'e kitchen. He's got a wed beard on his face. I don' yike mans wif wed beards!"

"Indeed, little master!" says carotty cabby. "Now, Lively!"

"Lively's yike a map all over her, is'nt she?"

says Baby. "All yose yittle, gwate big vein-places. An' how boo'fully you can see her bones shinin' frough! It's nice not to be stout, is'nt it? Mr. Marsden's stout—vewy; an' I don't yike his breard. I'se yikes shinin's man! I'se got a noo shinin' shinnin' in my pockie. I'se goin' to buy a big, garruping pony wif my shinnin' for Car'l. Car'l yoves 'e Baby!"

"Who-a, Lively! Now, little master; yon's th'ouse you're bound for!" and cabby lifts Baby in his big sinewy arms from the high box seat on to the pavement.

"'See them big doors? Go right in there, an' ring the bell. Pull hard!"

"Esh, man," says Baby gratefully; "I'se yike 'oo, man. Has 'oo got anybody ense?"

But cab and cabby were rattling away out of hearing. Baby is alone in the world.

One-half of the big doors is open. He makes his way bravely into a nice walled-in garden, down the drive, stopping a moment on his way to try to stroke a white Angora cat who won't be stroked, and who hurries off into the shrubbery in a huff.

Then Baby climbs the steps at the hall-door,

and rings the bell with a giant effort. The result frightens him. On and on that bell goes —tingle, ringle, tingle—as it would never stop, and as if the whole of the inside of the house must be a grand net-work of bells.

Baby looks round him at the big garden, the tall trees, and the high wall; then on tiptoe up at the big house. He can't even see up to the roof. It must be somewhere near the clouds— perhaps a sort of Jack-and-the-Beanstalk house. It is to be hoped there are no giants in the attics!

How big everything is here! In the presence of so much bigness, Baby feels as if he had suddenly grown very small himself — quite shrunk into his shoes, in fact!

And he felt so big and brave a little time ago!

What is mother doing, and Caryl? Will they be sorry that he has gone to be the lady's little boy? Of course mother knows all about it. She always does seem to know everything. Mother would tell him to be kind—to go and be the lady's little boy, because she had got "nob'dy ense." He will go. But a sob bursts from the poor little lips; Baby rubs his eyes very hard, and murmurs:—"He's weddy soddy for 'e poor yady; but he does want his own mover an' Car'l. Car'l yoves 'e Baby."

Just then the door opens and in a quick Jack-in-the-box sort of way, and there stands a big footman who stoops himself down a very long way before he can get on a tolerable level with poor little three-year-old.

"What is it you want, little master?" he asks kindly.

"He wants mover—no; he wants 'e yady," says Baby, firmly, but with trembling lips.

"Is it Mrs. Doran you want?"

"Esh," repeats baby; "Id's Mrs. Dorwan, s'e wented away in 'e cab, and he's tumin' to be her yitten boy. S'e's not got nob'dy ense!"

"Well, I never!" says the tall footman, and he draws himself up again to his full height. "There's some mistake, depend upon it; but you'd better come in or you'll be lost. Mrs. Doran's just gone out again, but you shall wait for her a bit in the drawing-room."

"S'e yikes yunning," remarks Baby, as he goes with the footman; "he hadn't got no bref wif yunnin' after her!"

The drawing-room is big and lofty. T[here]
are queer-shaped looking-glasses, and a [great]
many pictures and bits of china on the w[alls.]
It strikes Baby at once that all the chair-co[vers]
would make a good match with the gow[n]
which he saw Mrs. Doran last.

The footman leaves Baby with a plate of p[ink]
and white biscuits; and, after a tour of [dis-]
covery round the room, our hero, who is hung[ry,]
subsides into an easy-chair, and munches a[way]
comfortably enough.

"S'e's a weddy yong time," he remarks alo[ud,]
after about a quarter of an hour has gone b[y.]
"S'e's yike Kate, on'y Kate does'nt yik yunni[ng]
an' 'e yady does!"

The door opens, and in comes his "yady"
herself.

"Bless us!" she says nervously, when s[he]
catches sight of Baby, "James told me there w[as]
a child here, but I'd no idea that he'd left it b[y]
itself, with all my good china about! Let [me]
see—where have I seen you before?"

"In 'e dwoining room—wif mover," says Ba[by]
softly. "He's weddy soddy 'cos you's got n[o]
b'dy ense. He's tryen' to be oo's yittle boy[,]

but "—and his voice trembles a little—" he don't yike havin' no more mover, an' no more Car'l to yove 'e Baby!"

"What can have put such a strange notion into your head, I wonder!" says the lady sharply: "I don't like babies. Does your mother know where you are?"

"He 'spec's mover knows," says Baby, with a lump in his throat; "mover's weddy clever. Mover would tell 'e Baby to be kin'."

"You'll give your mother a terrible fright, I expect, wondering what's become of you, child," says the lady, in what seems to Baby a very cross voice. "And how in the world I'm to get you safe home I'm sure I don't know! Where do you live?"

"Wif mover," says Baby sadly.

"Yes, but *where*?"

"In e' big street, in 'e house wif mover an' awn of yem."

"What's your name?"

"Baby sometimes, but Noel awnways, 'cos he's kissened Noel. Carl calls 'e Baby a 'kissmas box."

"But your surname, child?"

"He hasn't got nuffin' more," says poor Baby; "but Cuff an' Carl an' Osif have got some more names. Cuff is goin' to codidge!"

"Well, I'm sure I don't know what to do with you," says the lady, laying her hand on her forehead to think. "I haven't the very faintest notion of where you live, and you are not much clearer on the subject yourself. Stop—I know! Mr. Marsden is coming to dine here to night, and *he'll* be sure to know who you are. I believe he knows the ins and outs of every child in the town."

"He's got a breard," falters Baby; "I'se don' yike to be kissed wif 'e breards."

"You do know Mr. Marsden then? Well, that's all right. I only hope to goodness that your parents may not have gone out of their minds, and been carried to the lunatic asylum before we can get to know where you live, and drive you home. *How* did you make your way here, child?"

"In 'e cab," explains Baby. "He sawed 'oo, an' he was yunnin' to catch 'oo, but he couldn', an' 'e kin' mans tooked him on a cab wif a horse wot was cawned Lively. He's tummed, 'cos 'oo's not got nob'dy ense."

"I'm sure I ought to be very much obliged to you for your consideration, child," says Mrs. Doran coldly; "but I do wish children wouldn't get hold of such fancies. It gives me a great deal of trouble. See now—it's just two o'clock. I'll ring, and my maid shall make you tidy for lunch."

"Esh," says Baby, in a subdued voice.

So the bell is rung, and Fidèle, the maid, carries off Baby into the upstair regions. He goes with a wistful backward glance at his "yady."

"I wis' s'e would be kin'," his beating little heart says to itself.

But Mrs. Doran does not even look up at him.

Presently Fidèle comes down to the drawing room again.

"If you please, madame—"

"Well?" says Mrs. Doran impatiently.

"Madame, ze foots of ze leetle boy are swoollen so bad and become so sore with his running. I have taken off his boots; what can I procure him for shoes?"

"I will come in a minute and see."

When she comes, Baby is sitting in an easy

chair, with his two little legs dangling down from it, all red and swoollen.

"His foots is weddy hot an' ill," Baby is saying to Fidèle, as Mrs. Doran comes in. "'E yady did yun so fast. He had'nt any breaf!"

"Poor child!" his "yady" says, surprised into a tone of real pity, as she sees the pain the little fellow must be suffering; then she adds sharply. "Whatever possessed you to play such a mad prank! Fidèle, run for some warm water, a sponge, and my cold cream."

Then she bathes the tired little feet herself, and puts on the cooling ointment.

"Id's weddy nice!" says Baby contentedly; "'Oo's weddy kin' now. I wis' 'oo was always kin'."

"Now, what to do for shoes, I don't know; unless—Ah, yes! Fidèle, you may go. I wish to finish the child myself."

And Mrs. Doran brings out of her wardrobe a small parcel, with a sweet scent about it. It contains a pair of tiny blue knitted slippers.

Baby's quick eyes see her stoop down and kiss both little shoes tenderly.

"Yat's what mover does to my s'oes," he says. "Whose is yose yittle s'oes?"

"A little boy's," says Mrs. Doran.

"Whose was 'e yitten boy!" pursues Baby.

"Mine."

"Yen 'oo *has* got someb'dy ense," says Baby joyfully. "He's weddy gwad!"

"No; the little boy is dead now."

"Is 'oo weddy soddy!" inquires Baby gently.

There is no answer, but a big tear splashes down hotly on to Baby's one leg, then on to the other.

"Yat's funny!" he says amused. "'Oo's kwyin' first on one of his yegs, an' then on 'e udder! I sink 'oo is soddy yat oo's little boy is deaded."

Mrs. Doran only covers her face with her hands, and Baby can see that she is crying very much.

He waits for a second, uncertain what to do. Then he throws his two soft, fat little arms round his "yady's" neck, and "poors" her, as he does mother at home.

"I'se goin' to be 'oo's yittle boy," he whispers. "Don' kwy—I'se don' yike kwyin'!"

A moment later, and Mrs. Doran is sitting in the easy chair, with Baby perched on her lap, and her arms round him. Her hard ugly face has suddenly become very soft and tender, and her eyes are quite red with crying. She is letting Baby look at a little face in her locket—the likeness of the little boy who used to wear the blue shoes.

At lunch, Baby sits close to his "yady," chattering away to her about "Car'l" and all of them at home.

The servants wonder, and can hardly believe their eyes, to see their stern, unloving mistress so mild and gentle, so much interested in the simple chatter of a child.

When Baby goes to have his hands and face washed after lunch, Mrs. Wadsom, the housekeeper, feels bound to come upstairs and express herself on the subject to Fidèle.

"Eh, and isn't it wondersome," she says, "to see my mistress so taken with a child!"

"It is a child of benediction, I do not doubt," says Fidèle; "and the good angel of Madame bade her be kind. He will do her a great good, the little one!"

"Well," says Mrs. Wadsom, "I'll tell you this Fidèle. I've never known her cry a tear, nor speak a word to any bairn, since her little Stanislaus died about the age of this, and that must be ten years ago now. She seemed to turn like a stone."

"He's soddy, 'cos 'e yady's not got nob'dy 'ense," says Baby. "He yoves 'e yady."

And true it is that Baby's love and sympathy have melted the ice of years. For simple love is like summer sunshine, and sympathy is like those soft spring breezes that open the coy little blossoms.

"'Et's go out in 'e garden," proposes Baby on his return from Fidèle's hands, fresh and bonnie.

"Very well," says his "yady" readily, "if your poor feet can walk there. We will pay a visit to the strawberry-beds—shall we? Hawkes here is rearing some very choice specimens in a frame for the fruit-show."

"Does 'oo yike st'awbayies?" inquires Baby, limping across the soft velvety lawn. His feet hurt him far more than he will own.

"Yes, very much I like them."

"O-oo-ooh!"

Baby gives a shrill little scream of delight.

There before him are the long beds, and the great red berries playing hide-and-seek under their cool green vines. The ground is strawberries; the very air is strawberries. It is a child's paradise.

"Now, take as many as you want; I'm glad you like them," says Mrs. Doran, pleased to see Baby's joy.

"Put them into your mouth, child—straight!" For Baby is filling his tiny hands, and crushing the ripe berries into jelly.

"He's gadderin' yem for 'oo," says Baby. "He's gwad 'oo yikes yem."

"No, no! Put them in your own mouth, child. When you have had as many as you want, you may gather a few for me."

"He win gadder 'e big-biggest of awn of yem for 'oo!" protests grateful Baby, filling his mouth with the luscious fruit.

"He sees *one—free—twenve—a hundred—minion* boo'ful st'awbayies in 'e flame yere," murmurs the young man, furnishing himself with a second relay of fruit. "He win gadder yem awn for 'e yady!"

"A fine growing day for your strawberries,

Hawkes!" says Mrs. Doran, going up to inspect the frame where the gardener is busy weeding.

"Ye-es, ma'am; ye-es!" says Hawkes, touching his hat nervously several times. "They be doin' oncommon well, they be!"

Hawkes is not used to having his mistress speak to him, except to give her orders in a haughty peremptory tone. He feels quite uncomfortable in this new order of things.

"He wis' Car'l could have some nice st'awbayies!" says Baby, taking into his rosy little mouth relay No. 10; Car'l yoves 'e st'awbayies, an' Car'l yoves 'e Baby."

"Then Caryl shall have some strawberries;" says Mrs. Doran; "and all the rest: I don't know how many there are of them. Hawkes, you may gather a good basketful of the ripest and finest, and send them up to the house."

"I sink 'oo's weddy kind," says Baby; making his way from the strawberry-beds to the frame, from which Hawkes has retreated to do his mistress's behest. "Does 'oo often have 'e yittle boys an' girns to eat 'e wipe st'awbayies?"

"O dear me, no! Never!" replies Mrs. Doran.

"They would trample down all the vines, and do dreadful damage I don't like children."

"Don' 'e yittle boys an' girns yike 'e wipe st'awbayies?" inquires Baby.

"I daresay they do. Now, Baby, I want you to stay here by yourself a moment. Don't get into mischief. I am going up to the house to tell James to send Mr. Marsden out to us in the garden directly he comes."

"He's weddy trustive, mover says!" says Baby; "Esh, wif his breard." Then, as his "yady" departs, Baby says gladly—

"Now he can make a boo'ful *s'prise* for 'e yady, an' get 'e wipe-wipest st'awbayies in 'e flame for her!"

The frame is left open to the sun, so it is quite easy to get at those tempting red berries—perfect giants by the side of even the biggest in the beds.

Snap goes the proud stalk of the king amongst them. Then comes the turn of the next in size, and the next. Those three make a handful for Baby.

"He can't hold any more st'awbayies in his two hands," says the little fellow, toddling off to the gardener. "He wants a gwate big cabbage yeaf to hold yem, man."

"A cabbage-leaf, young master? Very good!"

And Hawkes leaves his work to cut a cabbage-leaf for Baby.

"My! you *have* managed to get fine ones!" he exclaims, when he sees Baby's store.

"Yem's for 'e yady," says Baby joyfully.

"Wherever did you find 'em, little master? 'strikes me I needn't trouble to frame berries for 'xibitin' if such as them's to be growed i' the ground."

"He's got yem in 'e flame!" exclaims Baby eagerly. "Come an' gadder yem. Yere's a yot more growing in 'e flame!"

"In the frame,—*the frame!*" repeats poor Hawkes, staggering towards it in a dazed sort of way. "You don't mean to say that them berries——"!

But Hawkes never finishes that sentence of his. Dismay seizes his gardener's soul, for he sees that it is indeed sorrowfully true: his best and finest berries—his main hope for the exhibition—are lying hopelessly in Baby's cabbage-leaf.

"Those children! Those children!" he groans at last. "I'd never have thought it of my mistress! To have children in the garden when there's choice fruit about—and above all, such babies as ought to be keeping their cradles by rights! I couldn't have believed it of her. And now, whatever she'll say I'm sure I don't know!"

"'Oo's yike 'e yady," says Baby; contentedly surveying his trio of giants in the cabbage leaf, beautifully unconscious of the unmendable mischief he has done. "S'e don' yike 'e chindwen, but s'e yikes 'e Baby. Does 'oo yike 'e Baby?" he adds, turning his sunny little face up towards the gardener's rugged, grave one. "'Cos he yikes 'oo, man!"

"'Taint *your* fault. You're right enough," says Hawkes, with a severe glance at the luckless berries, as if they were in some way to blame for having allowed themselves to be picked and carried off. "It's put th' exhibition out of question though."

"An' I sink 'oo's wight enough, man," echoes Baby sweetly.

Poor Hawkes is standing shaking in his shoes beside the unfortunate frame, when Mrs. Doran and Mr. Marsden come down the garden shortly after. Baby trots straight up to his "yady" with his leaf, and presents it to her with great glee.

"He's gotted awn 'e biggest ones in 'e frame!" he announces.

To Hawkes' utter amazement, there is only a moment's frown on his mistress's face; then she actually smiles, and eats the poor ill-used berries with great relish.

"Why, Baby Noel!" exclaims Mr. Marsden, "What brings you here—independent young three-year-old as you are?"

And poor Baby has to submit to the kissing process he so much dislikes.

"He's tummed 'cos 'e yady's not got nob'dy ense," explains Baby with dignity. "But he was weddy soddy 'cos he not got any more mover an' Car'l. He's gettin' gwad now, 'cos he's got awn 'e st'awbayies."

"I see! You like strawberries better than mother an' Caryl," says Mr. Marsden laughing.

"He can't put mover an' Car'l into his mouf," argues Baby stoutly. "St'awbayies is weddy good."

"So they are," says Mr. Marsden; "especially with cream and sugar; eh, Baby?—Mrs Doran, this is one of the young Mayhews of No. 2, the Grove. You know Mrs. Mayhew—Col. Mayhew's wife. I expect she will be getting uncommonly anxious to know what has become of her young hopeful."

"So she will," says Mrs. Doran, with a sigh. "But I can't tell you how loth I feel to parting with the child. I'm not a kidnapper of babies by nature, as you know. But he isn't like other children. He's a creation to himself. Hawkes, tell them to have the closed carriage ready as soon as possible."

"Every-one of the Mayhew tribe are nice," says Mr. Marsden warmly. "But I think Caryl is my prime favourite. Such a sensible, merry, happy-go-lucky, light-hearted, good boy."

"Car'l is his fav'wet too," says Baby. "Car'l yoves 'e Baby."

"I must get to know them all," says Mrs. Doran pleasantly. "Baby will you come and see me very often?"

"Free-four-firty-hundred-minion times!" volunteers Baby heartily; "An' see 'e st'aw-bayies too!"

"Cupboard love, you see!" says Mr. Marsden; and they both laugh.

When the carriage comes round, his "yady" wraps Baby up, puts him in beside the strawberry basket, gives him a tiny note for mother, and says good-bye with a face like that with which she put on the little blue shoes.

"Why, s'e's kwyin' again!" exclaims Baby, marvelling at his "yady's" tearfulness. "S'e yikes kwyin', an' 'e old yadies yiked yarfin'!"

At home, too, Baby finds everybody crying, but not as if they liked it.

They all cluster round Baby like a swarm of bees, and he feels himself quite a hero.

"What a naughty Baby," says mother, hugging him to her; "to get out of the perambulator, and run away! You might have been run over and killed, my pet! How thankful I am to God that I have you safe home again."

And grannie whispers softly—"Children, children, let us all kneel down and say three 'Hail Maries' in thanksgiving."

And Baby's little piping voice rings out above all the rest, till they cry again for joy at hearing it.

Then mother reads her note, and Baby's tongue rattles on as if it never could tell all it has to tell of his wonderful adventures, especially that of cabby and the lean horse, and of the giant strawberries.

"Baby's weddy gwad he's got his mover, an' Car'l, and awn of yem again!" says that young gentleman, stroking mother's thin cheek with his soft little paw.

"And mother has'nt got words to tell how glad she is to see her Baby again safe and sound," says mother, in a shaky voice.

"When Kate came back without him, she sent the police to look for him; and she sent men out to all the friends she could think of, to ask if he was there; but they all came back saying 'not there.' Mother's heart very *nearly* got broken in two, Baby!"

"He's weddy soddy," says Baby penitently.

"Yes, you may well be sorry, young scamp!" says Caryl, pulling Baby's goldi-locks. "You've caused a pretty hubbub all over the town to-day. Everyone was crying out 'Child lost, stolen, or strayed—five pounds reward.' We didn't know you were worth five pounds until we'd lost you!"

"He's worf a shinin' shinnin' wot gwaunie gaved him," says Baby triumphantly.

"Directly she heard you were lost, Osyth set to work, and got heaps of brandy, and camphor, and sugar, and blankets ready," says Aloysius. "I propose we eat the sugar in honour of your having turned up safe."

"O, Al., you greedy boy!" snubs Daisy.

"Moonie proposed to have the pond dragged," says Cuth. solemnly. "It seemed rather a more practical idea than usual, until she remembered that there is no pond to drag!"

"How unkind, Cuth.!" says Moonie gently. "It's what people always do in such cases in story books. Kennie and Edie did most to bring Baby back safe. They said a whole rosary between them."

"And Kate tried to mend matters, and escape a scolding by going off into hysterics," says Caryl. "Girls are an awfully good hand at that sort of thing!"

"Magdalen dear," says gentle grannie to mother, "just look at that dear child's legs. I am sure they must be terribly painful."

And mother looks, shakes her head; and then

she and Osyth go upstairs to doctor the poor little legs that ran so fast out of kindness to his "yady."

"S'e' not got nob'dy ense," he whispers, with a little sigh, as mother takes off the blue knitted shoes.

CHAPTER VI.

MASTER ME.

"Me's coming to-day," Bruno announces to the Mayhew tribe, about a fortnight after Baby's little escapade. "I had a letter from him inside mother's. Granny says he'd have been here before, only he's been staying with Aunt Bee in Scotland. Of course, a fellow could'nt say so, but I'm sure I wish she'd keep him altogether!"

"For shame, Bru. !" says Osyth, shaking her small womanly head at him; "I think you are dreadfully prejudiced against poor Me, and very uncharitable too. Why, he's had time to grow into quite a nice boy since we all saw him. Besides, he's our cousin, so we must try to be fond of him, and not to hurt grannie's feelings. She thinks nobody in the world is so good as her Me."

"And if he is a cousin," retorts Bruno crossly, "we can't help that. I wish we could have had a say in the matter! But so are Aunt Bee's children our cousins; we'd be glad enough to have them. But *Me*—he's a perfect pig!"

"Calm yourself, dear man;" counsels sober Cuthbert. "It's never any good crying over spilt milk. And its well to be perfect in something, if only in piggishness."

"Poor Bruno!" says Caryl; "It is the remembrance of the old grievance that stings, is'nt it? He remembers how master *Me* made him fag for him all day long last time, just because Bru. is two year's younger than his lordship. I must say I don't like to see a fellow quite so cocksy, myself!"

"Al.'s old cocksie has bited Baby's toad wif his teef," puts in Baby. He has been on the look-out for something à propos to say for some time. "He's bited his yeg, an' 'e po'r toadie is kite yame!"

"Put the toad's leg into splints," suggests Caryl mischievously.

"I do wonder that you and the twinnies care for such ugly, slimy creatures," says Al. "Now my fowls are ten times as nice, and really useful. That old Brahma lays nearly every day now."

"O the dear, darling, delicious toads!" cry the twins, roused to defend the honour of their pets. "You can't think how nice and loving they are. Mine spit a kiss at me this morning, and when you hold them tight in your hands, you can feel their little hearts beat!"

"Our Ketchwayo got very tired lately, and moped behind a big stone until to-day," says Edie.

"But this morning," adds Kennie, "he ripped his shabby old brown coat all up the back, and underneath was such a beautiful shiny new one."

"Quite a go-to-meeting coat!" says Edie. "And what do you think he did with his old clothes?"

"Buried them," suggests Daisy.

"Packed them up by way of extra wraps for next winter," says Aloysius.

"Turned charitable, and handed them over to a poor relation," says Cuth.

"He had yem *for his dinner!*" cries Baby who has been a wondering witness of Ketchwayo's performance.

"Do you know, he actually did!" says Kennie. "He rolled up his old coat into a nice tidy bundle — and jumped at it, and swallowed it whole."

"Ugh!" says Bruno; "and you call that *nice* of him, do you? I call it very disgusting, but just what one might expect of an old Zulu."

"Economical, anyhow," says Cuth.; "it saves tailors' bills. I suppose toads are generally of an economical turn of mind. I've heard that they hardly ever eat—will live a thousand years or so fasting, quite comfortably sealed up in the hole of a rock! Now, to leave the toad subject, who feels inclined for a stroll into the country bird-nesting? I've several sets I want to perfect in my egg-collection before I go to Stonyhurst. I thought we'd leave the martins' nests in peace until to-morrow. Me can be with us then, and we'll make up a little picnic for him. It's a glorious place, the Gulch—all great red rocks, and water-falls trickling down them. Now, who'll go with me to-day?"

"Jolly! I will," volunteers Caryl.

"And all of us"—the "us" means Moonie, Al., Daisy, and Bruno. The twins go off to adopt Caryl's doubtful counsel with regard to the lame toad.

Osyth and Baby put on their sun-hats, and take grannie out for a gentle stroll in the garden.

And now seems the time to hear a little about the aforesaid Me Stanley, who is soon to appear upon the scenes.

Me lives with grannie when he is not at school. He has a father and mother, but they are both in India. Me was born in India, but when he was two years old, his father, Col. Stanley, brought him to England to live with grannie. Me knows nothing of his parents, except what he learns from the long letters they write by every mail to grannie and himself. He has just a dim remembrance too of the scarlet regimentals with gold facings in which he once saw his father.

Me is a very tall, handsome boy for his age, which is only ten. Grannie is quite wrapped up in him, and Me loves dear, sweet grannie with some sort of a more or less "cupboardy" love. Do you know what I mean?

Well, of course, Me would love such a grandmother, you say. But I assure you, in Me's case, it is not at all *of course*. The fact is, Me answers to his name. He is very particularly fond of No. 1; and people who put up a little altar in their hearts to that individual, have not generally much love to spare for anyone else.

Me is selfish—Oh, very selfish! I am sorry to have to say it; but you know, though I am telling you a story, I must do my best to tell you the truth at the same time.

Grannie can't see that he is so selfish—oh, dear no! She thinks Me just the pink of perfection, and he quite agrees with her. It seems to me that whenever grannie looks at Me she puts on her blue spectacles, and so she can't see his faults. It is a great pity, a very great pity; for, if one won't see the holes in one'self, and somebody else can't see them for us faithfully and lovingly, how are we ever to set about mending them?

Me's real name is Meredith, after his father; Me is only his every-day name. Meredith is like

Me's best velvet suit with silver buttons—it only comes out on high days and holidays. When Me writes to his parents in India, he signs himself Meredith sometimes—but only sometimes; for, though he likes to be grand, Meredith is a great deal of trouble to write, and takes up a whole line to itself in Me's big, sprawling copper-plate.

The children are all at luncheon when their expected visitor arrives. Baby's quick ears are the first to hear the cab stop at the hall-door.

"Yere's Me's caddidge tum, gwannie!" he says.

And very soon after Me is amongst them; his bonnie face rosy and browned by the sunshine that plays on the heathy Scotch moorlands.

"My darling Me!" cries grannie, holding out her arms to him.

Me does not seem to see the dear old lady, but is past her and by Aunt Magdalen's side in a moment, being kissed and questioned about Aunt Bee, Uncle Frank, and the children.

"I'm awfully hungry," he remarks at last, sitting down between Baby and Cuth., where a place has been left for him; "though I've got through any amount of sandwiches on the way. Hey, Baby! You're new since I was here last."

Baby submits to be kissed, with a flushed little face. Me's neglect of grannie has gone to the little fellow's heart.

"He's never kissed his gwannie!" he says in a low tone, full of reproach. "Baby will kiss gwannie for Me." Down slips Baby from his tall chair, and grannie feels two soft arms round her neck, while he bestows upon her cheek several kisses more or less sticky after the jam pudding he has been eating.

"Dear Baby!" says grannie. "Why did you do that?"

"'Cos 'oo's got nob'dy ense to kiss 'oo," says Baby, going back to his place.

"Now *Me* kiss gwannie!" urges Baby softly.

Me pretends to be too much taken up with his dinner to hear.

"Me's senfish," says Baby, in the same low voice. "Baby have a time wif him!"

Me fidgets uncomfortably in his chair, and wishes Baby somewhere near Jericho.

"Me yikes his dinner better yan gwannie," continues Baby softly.

"Go on with your dinner, Baby dear, and don't talk," says mother.

Baby subsides.

"I say, Me," says Cuthbert, "we were thinking of making up a jolly picnic to the Gulch to-morrow. You know where that is, don't you?"

Me nods.

"I'm sick of picnics and midges," growls ten-year-old Me. "There've been nothing but picnics and talk about picnics since I've been up with Aunt Bee. The children are wild after them."

"Ah, but you'll enjoy this," says Al. "Cook makes really good stuff to take with us."

"There's nothing to do at a picnic but eat," says Me.

"Ah, but there'll be lots to do at this one," says Caryl. "We are all going to try to find some sand-martins' eggs for Cuth. He wants to make up his collec' before he's off to Stoneyhurst. I expect it will be too early to find as many as we want, so it'll be good fun hunting them up."

"Cuthbert has a collection of birds' eggs, then?" says Me eagerly. "Oh, Cuthbert, let me see them; will you?"

"By all means," says Cuth. good-naturedly. "Do you collect yourself?"

"No; but I've made up my mind to, right away. Have you any spare eggs to give me?"

"Al. comes in for all I have to spare," says Cuthbert. "He's getting a pretty good show by degrees."

"I say, you'll turn them over to me, won't you now, Aloysius—there's a good fellow?" begs Me.

"Don't you wish you may get 'em!" says Al., not unkindly, however.

"Won't you come and say a word to me, darling?" pleads granny, whose wistful, loving eyes have followed Me ever since he came in. "I have'nt seen you for so very long. Have'nt you any messages for me from Uncle Frank and dear Auntie Bee?"

"I'm going to see Cuthbert's eggs, grannie," says Me. "Won't another time do for a talk. I can't remember the messages just now."

"The eggs can wait, of course, if grannie wants you," says Cuthbert gravely.

"Oh no, dear!" says gentle grannie. "I can ave a talk another time. Go and see Cuth.'s eggs, darling. They are beautiful, and dear Cuth. has taken such pains with them. He showed me them all yesterday—but I was too stupid to remember the long Latin names."

"Me's not said his gwace," remarks Baby, as that young gentleman goes off with Cuthbert. "Baby win say his gwace for him."

The little hand makes the sign of the cross very reverently, and Baby says grace twice over —once for himself, once for Me.

Me looks back and sees it all, and a feeling near akin to dislike rises in his heart against poor innocent Baby.

"What an *awfully* good Baby that is!" he says to Caryl. "He'll take a lot of snubbing to put him in his proper place, it seems to me!"

"If you're going to abuse Baby, you'd better not come to any of us—least of all me," answers Caryl gaily. "'Car'l yoves 'e Baby,' you know! Go to old Nanna, if you've anything to say against him, and fight a duel with her. I'd back old Nanna against you though, any day, where her Baby was in question!"

"Such babies ought to be kept in their

cradles!" says Me, from the superior height of his ten-and-a-half years.

"I'd just like to see you trying to keep Baby in his if he had one!" laughs Caryl. "You'd have a pretty hard task, I guess!"

"Hullo! Those are the eggs then," says Me, glad to change the subject; "Yes!—I can't say I think much of them. I'll soon have more. See if I don't!"

Cuthbert bites his lip, and opens the second drawer of rare and beautifully set English eggs.

"Those two smallest ones are grasshopper-warblers," he says with pride. "I was in luck that day. I came upon them in a big swampy meadow by the river-side. *Please* don't handle them, Me! They are very fragile, and I would'nt lose them for anything."

"I must hold them—just this once," persists Me. "Don't think I shall be such a butter-fingers as to break them. I've handled heaps of eggs before these!"

Crash!

"O! Bother! I've gone and done it. What stupid, thin things they are!"

"Oh, Me!" exclaims Caryl, in great distress;

"That's both the warblers. Poor Cuth.! Say you're sorry—quick!"

"I ain't," growls Me. "It was all his own fault. If he had'nt made a fuss, I should'nt have done it. And now he's in a wax!"

Cuthbert says nothing. He gathers together the broken egg-shells slowly, puts them into their place, closes the cabinet, and leaves the room.

"Poor old Cuth.!" says Bruno.

"For shame of yourself, Me!" bursts forth Al. "You've no more feeling than a cat. You might at least have said you were sorry. Why could'nt you have put them down when Cuthbert told you?"

"Po'r Cuff!" says Baby, coming up to the group; "He's kwyin', yocked up in his woom wif mover!"

"You're all of you a sulky lot," says Me angrily. "I shall go and find grannie."

"Gwannie's walkin' in 'e garding wif Puck," says Baby.

"That hateful dog!" growls Me, as he goes out.

"Well, Me, dear!" says Grannie, as that young

gentleman comes slowly towards her, "Come and walk with me if you are not too tired. I have been so longing for a chat with my boy. But, of course, your cousins will want to see all they can of you."

"I'm coming in a minute, Grannie," says Me. "Puck, Puck!"

The pug goes off at his call towards the stables. Presently Me comes back alone.

"What has become of Puck, dear?" says Grannie. "He was out here enjoying a stroll with me. He is so fat that old Grannie can keep pace with him comfortably."

"He's stupid," says Me. "Pugs have no sense. He gets in one's way so, too, and barks at everything. I've shut him up in the stable."

"What a pity!" says Grannie. "I like to have him with me, dear."

"Do you, Grannie?" says Me carelessly. "Have him when I'm not there then."

"You think I ought to be quite content with having my boy back, don't you, Me?" says gentle Grannie with a smile. "I am too."

"What selfish children those Mayhews are!" says Me crossly. "They're for ever quarrelling. And that Baby's such a prig!"

"The dear Baby! Everybody loves him," says Grannie warmly. "And the others all seem to be very nice, good children."

"And such a rubbishing collection of eggs," continues Me, "to make so much fuss about!— What time is it, Grannie?"

"Three o'clock, dear, by my watch."

"Then I'll tell you what I've made up my mind to do. We've had a bit of a squabble— not much, you know, Grannie, but enough to make us want to keep out of each others' way,—so I'll go out for a walk on my own account."

"Hadn't you better wait for the others, dear?" suggests Grannie.

"No," says Me. "They're cross."

And off he goes.

"Poor little Me!" sighs Grannie. "Only children always find it very hard to get on with others."

At the door Me meets Baby with a very radiant little face.

"He's got a yetter f'om his yady, an' it's a 'tation to tea, mover says!" he explains to Me.

"Get out of my way, Baby," says Me crossly.

"Don't 'oo want any st'awbayies?" inquires Baby sweetly.

"I don't want you," grunts Me, passing Baby and going out.

"Me don't yike st'awbayies," murmurs Baby. "Me's c'oss. Is peoples always c'oss when yey don' yike st'awbayies?"

And he trots off to the other children in the schoolroom.

"It's a yetter, an' a 'tation to tea wif 'e yady an' 'e st'awbayies," he cries excitedly.

"Hurrah!" exclaims Caryl. "Why, you are a lucky young dog, Baby. Your always getting invitations! What does mother say?"

"Mover says 'e caddidge win be weddy soon," says Baby, "for awn of us to go."

"Me will cheer up at the prospect of strawberries," says Al.

"Where is he?"

"Me's gone in 'e stweet," says Baby. "Me don' yike st'awbayies."

"Me's an odd fish," says Bruno. "Isn't he going then!"

"He's goned," says Baby.

"Where's Cuth.?"

"Here," says Cuth.'s gruff voice at the door. "Where's the boy—Me?"

"He's gone out, Baby says," says Osyth. "I don't think he feels very happy. You'll forgive him, won't you, Cuth.?" she adds pleadingly.

Cuthbert nods. He has had a hard struggle with himself, and his better self and his good angel have come off victors.

"Me must go with us," he says presently. "Which way did he go, Baby?"

"Down 'e countwy way," says Baby. "Me's c'oss."

"I'll go after him," says Cuth.

"O Cuth., then you'll miss the treat!" says Caryl dolefully.

"Never mind! You'll bring us some strawberries home, won't you?"

"Cuth., you're a brick!" exclaims Al. warmly.

"A *bath* brick, then," says Cuth., laughing as he goes out; "only good to rub and scrub with!"

Presently the carriage comes round and everybody piles into it.

"S'e's yookin' at us!" says Baby suddenly.

"Who is 'she,' Baby?" inquires Daisy; "the cat's grandmother?"

"Has 'Muts got a gran'mover?" exclaims Baby delighted. "It's one of 'e Yittle Sisters."

"Oh, then, Caryl, *do* ask John to stay a moment!" pleads Moonie. "I want to run in and fetch the vests mother let me knit for those poor old men. It is Sister Marguèrite, and she asked for them."

"All right," says good-natured Caryl; "we'll wait for you, Moonie, if you're back some time before next year! Sister Marguèrite, Magdalen has gone indoors to fetch some woollen things she's been making to keep your old men warm this summer," says mischievous Caryl.

"In 'e winter," corrects Baby.

"I am sure our old men will be very grateful for Magdalen's charity," says the Sister, setting down her basket to rest her arm.

"You look *so* tired, Sister," says Osyth. "Do go in and rest. Mother is there, and so's Grannie."

"Sister Catherine and I have had a long hot walk to-day," says Sister Marguèrite; "and our Lord has laid a few crosses on us by the way—painful to carry, but very sweet."

"'Et 'e Baby see 'oo's cwosses," says three-year-old.

"Thou can'st not see them, little one," answers Sister Marguèrite smiling.

"He would yike to kiss yem," says Baby.

"See this crucifix then, little one, and kiss it," says the Sister kindly. "It is a wonderful crucifix. Now is not time, or I could tell how it has been blessed to very many. I venerate it."

"I'se yike 'oo's cwoss," says Baby, pressing it to his lips.

"Here's Moonie!" exclaims Bruno, as the little girl arrives, breathless, and hugging a fat parcel in both arms.

"For the poor old men who were so cold last winter," she says. "Will you ask them to say some prayers for me?"

"Indeed they will, Magdalen," says the Sister. "God bless you all!"

"I'll be a little Sister some day, I think," says Moonie, after a long reverie.

"Then I'm sure I hope I shall never come to be one of your old men," says Al. decidedly. "You'd be up in the moon, and forget all about such worldly concerns as a fellow's dinner!"

"Baby be a yittle Sister some day, wif a cwoss," says Echo; whereupon everybody laughs.

These little expeditions to Rosemount House are by no means a rare thing now. Baby often receives a letter of invitation for the whole Mayhew tribe. At other times his "yady" begs Mrs. Mayhew to "lend her Baby for a day or two: she is really *hungry* for him." So Baby is packed up, Nanna cries over him—more or less according to the length of time he is to stay—and he goes to console his "yady."

Fidèle and Mrs. Wadsom, James and Hawkes, are almost as pleased to see Baby on these occasions as Mrs. Doran herself.

Fidèle says—" Ze pit-pat of his foots is sweet music in the house. He brings ze sunshine everywhere he goes—dis child of Benediction."

Baby has wrought wonderful changes at Rosemount House in this last fortnight.

" Yere's such a yot of f'owers on 'e yawn," he remarks one day. " Ye're weddy pwetty sings; but yere's no woom yeft for Car'l an' Baby an' awn of yem to p'ay nice'y."

" Hawkes, we'll have some of those extra flower-beds taken away, and grass-sods put down in their place," says Mrs. Doran next day. " There really are too many beds on the lawn, and the shrubbery-borders want more flowers."

"Yere's a yot of yittle chinds in 'e stweet wot would yike some st'awbayies," Baby ventures another day.

"Do you want them to come in here and have some, Baby?" asks Mrs. Doran.

"Esh," says Baby. "*Awn* 'e po'r yitten chinds. Yat would be nice!"

"Wadsom, you may bake plain plum-cakes for about eighty children," says Mrs. Doran next week. "I've arranged for the children of the Convent poor school to come here to-morrow for fruit and cake."

"Yere's no nice nurs'wy in 'e house," remarks Baby again. "He's got nowhere to put his toy-sings."

"Fidèle," says Mrs. Doran, we really must have a nursery. I wonder I never thought of it. That poor child must feel quite uncomfortable without one. Let me see—we must have plenty of bright pictures, toys, and a good rocking horse."

"Will Madame choose the back room for a childrens' chamber?" inquires Fidèle.

"Oh, no, Fidèle. That room gets no sun worth mentioning. I shall change my bedroom, and let him have that."

"Madame is good," says Fidèle warmly. "She will be to the little one like his mother."

But now it is time that we leave Rosemount House, where our Mayhews are pitching into their strawberries and cream with great zest, and overtake their cousin Me in his lonely walk. Cuthbert has not been able to find him, and it is no wonder that he cannot guess where Me is gone.

Once more Me is like his name—looking after No 1.

"I'll have a try after those old martins," he says to himself.

"They'll give all they get to Cuthbert to-morrow, depend upon it, as we ain't friends. So I'll be before hand, and see what I can find for myself."

A voice within whispers pretty loudly,— "Dont be mean."

"I'm not," answers Me. "They'll do their best for Cuth., and I must do the best for myself."

But alas, for Me's hopes! The martin's holes

in the rocks are many; many are the frightened little birds that fly out from them, and wheel round his head with shrill cries of defiance; but their eggs are safe from his hand, deep, deep, down in the rock.

Me pushes his arm in as far as it will go, only to bring it out again bruised and dusty.

At last he leaves the Gulch, and turns homeward in something uncommonly like a rage with himself and everybody and everything else.

Why can't those martins build their nests sensibly, where their eggs can be got at easily?

Why has he been so foolish as to waste his time and graze his arms, in trying to get what is'nt to be had?

Why are those Mayhew children so nasty and disagreeable with him, when he is such a nice, agreeable little boy?

Conscience tries to put in a word here; but Me shuts its mouth with—" Well, at all events, Grannie thinks so!"

Poor Me! His thoughts are not very happy or comfortable ones, as you will perceive; but he can't find any better, nor does his temper improve as he nears home.

Master Me.

Presently he comes to a little cottage, standing by itself. The narrow raised foot-path passes quite close to the door.

"Filthy hole for anyone to live in!" growls Me.

A little girl, about eight years old, is sitting in her chair before the door, singing hymns to amuse herself.

The path is narrow, and she is in Me's way. She must move her chair, or Me must step down on to the dusty road.

The child does not move aside, and Me's temper will not let him do so either.

"Get out of my way, child—quick!" he says rudely.

The little girl only stares at him stupidly, and stops singing.

"Get up, I say!" roars Me.

Still the child does not stir.

"Then I shall make you," cries Me angrily; and he pushes child and chair violently through the open door into the cottage. Over go both of them on to the floor; the little girl crying piteously; half with pain, half with fright.

"That'll teach you to keep out of people's way!" says cross Me.

"I'll tell Barney—I'll tell my brother!" sobs the child.

"Tell what you like—I don't care!" growls Me, as he goes on his way.

Round the corner Me comes suddenly upon Cuthbert, who has almost given up all hope of meeting him.

Me feels very uncomfortable. He would give a good deal to be able to get out of Cuth's way. He does'nt fancy having to eat humble-pie; though, by-the-bye, humble-pie is a most wholesome dish for any of us!

"Hallo, Me; old fellow!" cries Cuthbert, laying his hand kindly on the boy's arm; "There you are! I've been half the world over hunting you up. You've missed such a treat!"

"Humph!" grunts Me.

"The whole boiling of us were asked out to a strawberry-feast at Mrs. Doran's—Baby's friend, you know."

"Humph!" grunts Me again.

"I'm very sorry," says Cuth., trying to break the ice.

The grasshopper-warblers are in Me's mind.

"I'm glad," he growls.

"Are you *always* cross, Me?" says Cuth., laughing. "If—if you've got the warblers on your conscience, never mind them now! It's all forgiven and forgotten."

"It was all your own fault for fussing about them," snarls Me.

"Very well—we'll say I smashed them," says Cuth. good-naturedly. "Only cheer up, please, Me—you remind me of a Scotch mist! Where have you been, old fellow, all this afternoon?"

Me's cheeks tingle sharply, and he says nothing. He is beginning to see how mean he has been.

"Ah, well! You don't remember the names of our parts, I daresay," says Cuth. "It's nearly three years since you were here."

All that Cuthbert can say is of no avail. Me won't come out of his sulks, they have a silent, uncomfortable walk home together.

"Me's c'oss," says Baby that evening.

"Me's just the old piggie he always was!" says Al.

"Take care, Al. dear," whispers mother as she passes. "You know we may look in other people's looking-glasses sometimes, and see ourselves."

"I wonder what Me's been sent here for!" muses Moonie. "I suppose people are always brought together for some good or other."

"To make us all cross and disagreeable," says Bruno.

"To give us an opportunity of exercising a great deal of charity, and of winning a great many hard, brave victories over ourselves," says mother softly. "Don't let your opportunities slip, children."

"He won't 'et yem s'ip!" echoes Baby.

CHAPTER VII.

BEARS.

How long Master Me's sulky fits usually last, of course, there is no telling; but this one doesn't seem inclined to come to an end in a hurry.

Next morning dawns, bright and beautiful. Me comes down to breakfast like a cloud into the midst of sunshine. Everybody feels chilled. Grannie gets anxious, and inquires if her darling is unwell. Me growls out some sort of answer, and shrugs his shoulders.

"You seem sad and low-spirited, dear," ventures Grannie again. "Is anything the matter?"

"I only want people to let me alone," growls Me.

So they do let him alone, and Me doesn't look as if he relished his loneliness. The day drags on very slowly and drearily for him.

"The picnic! the dear picnic!" cries little Daisy that afternoon, in high glee. "I've watched cook filling the big baskets with no end of good things."

"I bags the biggest to carry!" says slangy Al.

"All right, old fellow," agrees Caryl. "Your shoulders are broader than mine."

"Baby bags carryin' 'e bigges' basket," says Echo.

"O Baby!" cries Osyth, catching the young gentleman in her arms, and giving him a toss up to the ceiling; "I'm sure you'll have more than enough to do to carry yourself all that way!"

"Isn't it time to start?" say the twins.

"Of course. No time like the present," remarks Cuth. sagely.

"Baby win s'ew Me 'e way," says Baby, as the party sets out.

"Me, will you carry the ladle?" says Cuth. "Cook always lends us one to poke out the eggs with. Those impudent martins take care to lay them in the very bottom of the tunnels they make."

"No, thank you," says Me, falling behind the rest.

"Baby an' Me's goin' a-gedder," says Baby charitably.

"No; come on, Baby!" says Caryl. "You'll only bother Me."

"P'or Me's not got nob'dy ense!" says Baby pityingly, still keeping to his cousin's side.

"Yes, he shall stay with me," says Me crossly. He is tired of solitude, and yet cannot make up his mind to join the party; besides a spirit of contradiction has taken possession of him. "You can all of you go on, and don't bother about us."

"Me's got someb'dy ense *now!*" says Baby, proud at Me's having accepted his company, but a wee bit shy of being left altogether to the tender mercies of his sulky cousin.

"Do you really mean it, Me?" says Osyth.

"Of course I mean what I say."

"But what if Baby gets tired?"

"I'll carry him, that's all."

"Do you think it's safe to trust him with Me, Cuth, dear?" whispers motherly Osyth.

"I think so," answers Cuth. "Perhaps he will bring Me to a better mind."

"It's a queer fad of Me's—this taking to Baby," says Caryl merrily. "He was running him down hard enough only yesterday."

So the party march on, leaving Me and Baby to follow in the rear.

And someone else is following Me all the time, dogging his steps, stealthily, noiselessly as a shadow. Me does not know it.

"Baby's bwought a yong stick for Me to poke 'e nests wif," Baby announces, when they reach the Gulch at last. "An' he's goin' to gadder some of yose yennow, an' gween, an' boo f'owers for mover hisself."

"Afterwards, Baby," says Me. "But now you must come and sit down. I'm tired, and those other fellows are all out of sight. Very polite of them, I must say! There's a cool place under this rock."

"It gives a golden flower for mover best," pleads Baby.

"And I like you to sit down. So come. It's not safe for you to be climbing about here by yourself."

"He's tumin'," says Baby, as he seats himself close to Me, with a bit of a sigh, and a wistful glance at the patches of golden dandelion overhead.

"Do you like to be frightened, Baby?" inquires Me lazily.

"He yikes Car'l to fwighten him, 'cos Car'l on'y pertends," says Baby.

"Because I'll tell you something to make a nice creepy feeling come over you. Listen!"

And selfish Me feels a keen pleasure as the little fellow presses up closer to him, a look of real terror in his face.

"It's about a brown bear," he begins.

"Baby don' yike 'e bears," says Baby fearfully.

"This bear was in the town yesterday, being shown about, and dancing with a great chain round his neck."

"Po'r bear!" says Baby; "wif a gwate chain wound his neck!"

"And somebody else was 'poor' too," continues Me. "There were a whole lot of children round, teazing the bear, because it couldn't reach them with its chain. When suddenly the chain broke, and the bear came on to them with a bounce!" And Me throws himself upon Baby to suit the action to the words.

"Baby don' yike that story," he says piteously with a little cry.

"Well, it will soon be done now. The bear got hold of one little boy. He didn't bite him, but he hugged him in his arms so fiercely, before the bear-man could catch him and get the child away, that they took him straight away to the hospital, and the doctor says he won't live very long."

"Is 'e bear goned wight away?" inquires Baby, glancing round him fearfully.

"No; I believe he's somewhere round," says Me maliciously. "I advise you not to go climbing about the rocks for flowers, that's all."

"For mover," says Baby sadly; "he wanted yem for mover. Will 'e bear come if Baby on'y gadders f'owers for mover?"

"I shouldn't think it will make much difference to him who you gather them for," answers Me lazily. "I say, I'm going to sleep, and you shall tell me a story to send me off. Now, then!"

"He can't ten storwys, 'cept to mover and Moonie!" says Baby tearfully. He is beginning to feel very miserable, what with Me, the bear-story, and no flowers for mother.

"Well, then, now tell *me* one. Be quick!" commands Me.

"Yen he must put on his finkin' cap," says Baby, in imitation of Moonie. "Once upon a time yere was a old cow—fifteen, twenty, minion years old!"

"My!" says Me, sleepily.

"An' 'e old cow had a little, wee, wee chind-cow. An' s'e gaved it some nice cakes for e' picnic, out of e' baskets. An' 'e yitten chind-cow was weddy good."

A pause.

"Well?" says Me, still more sleepily.

"An' yere were a gwate many big sheeps an yitten sheeps in 'e field—sixteen, fowsand, free years old! An' 'e yitten sheeps an' 'e big sheeps was awn good."

Another pause. Baby's flow of thought has failed him.

"Well," says Me, "let's hear what happened next, Baby?"

"Oh! 'E old cow gobbyned up 'e yitten sheeps; an' 'e big sheeps was fwightened. An' yey awn yunned away. An' e' yitten cow yunned away too. An' yey sawed a woonf tumin' out of 'e wood, wif teef, an' cal-laws, an' a gwate yong tain—nearny free mines yong! An' yey was fwightened. An' yey cwimbed up on to 'e top of a twee; an' 'e woonf cawned a yion, an' 'e yion cawned a bear; an' yey awn cwimbed up e twee. An' 'e p'or aminals yunned away. An' yey cwimbed up on to 'e church tower. An' 'e bears, an' 'e yions, an' 'e woonfs could'n' get yem."

"Is that all!" says Me drowzily.

"Yere's somesing more," says Baby puffing for breath. "Yen yey awn gobbyned each other up,—an' 'e woonfs, an' 'e bears, an' e' yions, an' 'e cows, an' 'e sheeps. An' yey was *awn* happy ever after. Yat's 'e end of 'e storwy."

"And, now I'm rested, Baby," says Me graciously. "So give me your stick, and w'ell go and see after the martins, and you can get your flowers for Aunt Magdalen."

"But yere's 'e bear!" says Baby timidly.

"Never mind him. Come!"

So the two scramble up the rock side. Baby's bare knees come in for a great many bruises and scratches by the way, but he would not for worlds complain of the smart.

At last they stand on the higher level, panting for breath. Gaunt red rocks are piled round and above them, on all sides but one; pierced with numberless round holes, into which mother martins are tumbling sleepily; for it is getting dusk, and high time that eggs and baby-martins should be tucked up for the night.

Down below the children are more rocks. Tiny streams trickle down their sides, making pleasant, fairy music, and the summer evening breeze sings a gentle wordless melody to it. There is lots of greenery too—shubbery, and even big pines here and there, and to the left a tangled thicket carpetted with nettles.

Baby soon fills his tiny hands with golden dandelions, ferns, and pimpernel, and Me goes after the aforesaid martins.

"All right, Baby?" he calls out presently.

"Esh, Me," replies Baby, echoing old Nanna. "He's gadderin' 'e f'owers — amoosin' hisself nice'y."

"That's right. Take care of yourself," cautions Me. "I'm coming soon, and we'll go to the others for something to eat. There's a kingfisher's nest here, it strikes me. I saw the old bird fly out."

"Where, Me?" cries Baby excitedly. "He's tumin' to see."

Me is making his way cautiously down the side of a rock. Beneath him is a large dark pool, awfully deep and still. The supposed nest is almost on a level with the water.

"Stay where you are, Baby," calls out Me.

"He's on'y stann'in' still an' yookin," answers Baby.

Me has almost reached the goal; almost,— when, suddenly the bushes beside the pool begin to quiver and rustle, as if some heavy body were forcing its way through them.

"Is yere a kin'fisser in 'e bushes?" cries Baby delighted.

Me does not answer. He clings to the rocks and listens anxiously.

Another rustle in the bushes, nearer this time. Then a long, low growl.

Me trembles, and his teeth chatter in his mouth for fear.

"Does'n 'e kin'fisser make a funny noise!" says Baby, much amused.

Me says not a word, but his face turns cold and white.

"It is the bear!" his poor little heart whispers, and there is no hope of escape. Me's time to die must be close at hand.

In a flash—a terrible flash—all Me's unkindness, sulkiness, and meanness of the last few days, and of all his life, shines upon him with a new, awful light—almost as God must see it! And a silent cry of shame, and sorrow, and repentance for his sins goes up straight from Me's heart. Ah, if he only might live to prove how different, how very different all the rest, of his life should be!

Another spring forward in the bushes, the unseen creature gives another horrid growl; Me feels that it is all over with him.

A little cry "Jesus, Mary, help!" then his poor hands, his whole body, grow numb and cold, he looses his hold of the rock, and falls into the dark, black pool below, struggling feebly for dear life.

"Me's going to be drowned!" cries Baby, in great trouble. "He was yookin' at 'e kin'fisser, an' he's tumbyned into 'e wiver. An' he's not got nob'dy but Baby to get him out. He's tumin' to save 'oo, Me. Never min'!"

And suiting the action to the word, dear little Baby throws aside his flowers, and begins to clamber down the rockside to save Me.

Who could expect that little three-year-old should reach the bottom safely, brave little climber as he is?

"He's tumin' weddy quick, don' be frightened, Me!" he repeats bravely.

"Don' you yike 'e col' water, Me!"

Poor little three-year-old! He has only made a few short steps, when his feet miss their footing, and down he goes into the black pool with a splash and a scream.

Will anyone save them? Can anyone hear that scream of distress?

The merry voices of the other children are coming nearer. They are calling the two truants to the meal they have got ready. But they will come too late. Before they can have time to reach the pool, those black waters must have closed for ever over the two cousins struggling so hopelessly in its depths.

Yes, someone hears!

At the very moment of Baby's fall, by some strange chance, Barney Wheelan is standing on the brink of the pool.

"Faith! I niver thocht iv it's goin' so hard wiv him!" he mutters; and down into the pool goes bare-footed Barney to the rescue. He swims like a fish. Me is soon safe on the bank, half fainting; and Baby, quite insensible.

"What'll he do wiv the two of ye?" says Barney puzzled.

"Shout, Barney; shout," whispers Me. "Tell them to come quick."

"Come quick wid ye, whoiver ye are!" shouts Barney; "for it's dhrowned intirely they are!"

Barney's call soon brings the Mayhew party to the spot.

Barney is kneeling, with Baby in his arms, and Me lying, half dazed upon the ground.

"Shure, an' they've been enjoying a bit iv a

wetting," explains Barney; "and its meeself has had a share in the same, bad luck to it!"

"O Baby, Baby! Poor mother!" cries Osyth; and her loving arms soon relieve Barney of his burden.

"Let us get home quick!" she says. "I can carry Baby until we meet a cab. Cuth., help Me; poor Me!"

"Shall we leave the baskets and things down there?" says Aloysius.

"It's meeself'll be pleased to be packin' thim, an' bringin' thim up to the house for ye," volunteers Barney.

And as the sad little party turn away, he mutters between his teeth. "Shure, it's me heart that's throubled for the babby—who'd have thocht he have thried to have saved the ither one? But it's no more than the boy deserved, at all, at all, bad luck to him! An' she jist dyin' away before me eyes for him—the little baste!"

Fortunately, not very far from the Gulch, the children meet Mrs. Doran returning from a drive in the country. Of course she takes them all into the carriage, and drives them home at once.

She lets Baby lie in her lap, and says nothing, but tears fall in showers on the poor little unconscious face.

"It is an angel, Madame," says Fidèle, who is with her mistress.

"It cannot be long for our cold world, this child of Benediction. It seems to me that he bears heaven in his sweet face."

But God does not always take our best and sweetest. Earth is his garden as well as heaven, and He leaves us a few beautiful flowers here and there to adorn it, and fill it with innocent perfumes.

CHAPTER VIII.

THE NUN'S CROSS.

What I am going to tell you now is quite true; and, as you listen, let your heart thank God who still shows wonderful things to the simple babes and sucklings, whilst He hides them from the wise.

Barney comes up to the house with the remains of the unfortunate picnic, and a very rueful face that night.

"How is the boy and the babby?" he asks nervously.

"Master Me seems not much the worse, but Baby is very bad," the servants say.

"Could I spake to the Misthress thin?" inquires Barney, wriggling uncomfortably.

"Mistress is with Baby, and won't leave him for anyone. Won't some other time do for you."

"No," says Barney; "But may be I could spake wid the young misthress?"

So Osyth comes down to see Barney.

Poor Barney bows, and bows again, and twists his cap in his fingers, but can't get out what he wants to say.

"Well, Barney, what is it?" says Osyth; "don't be afraid to speak."

"Shure ye'll be affther sendin' poor Barney to prison," says the lad nervously; "but he must spake, an' that's the thruth."

"Why, Barney, we can only be very grateful to you," says Osyth, astonished at the boy's manner. "You saved my little brother's life and my cousin's too. If you had'nt been there, they would both have been drowned. I am sure we are very grateful to you, and if you come up to-morrow, mother will give you something."

"I'm not affther begging a thrifle," says Barney, fidgetting again. "There ain't much merit in makin' folks dhrown for the pleasure in gettin' thim out of their disthress, at all!"

"But you never put them into the water Barney," says Osyth. "You know my cousin heard a growling noise in the bushes. He thought it must be the bear that was being shown in the town; and he was so frightened that he fell in. And our dear little Baby fell in, too, through trying to save him."

"It was meself was the bear," says Barney, hanging his head. "Was'nt it that boy that threw me little sisther out of her chair, lame as she was, an' she took such a pain an' fright that she's dying, an' may be dead before Barney gets home agin? An' wasn't it meself that said to meself, 'I'll see the vengeance on him, for murtherin' of her?'"

"Oh Barney!" says Osyth very much shocked.

"An' it's the whole thruth," says Barney.

"An' I sees the bear in the streets, an' says I to meself, says I—'Its the bear shall do it! and I followed him, the sulky baste, to the pool, and I got behind the bushes, and I growled at him. Shure I niver thocht he'd fall in, an' the babby go affther him; but I'd give him a frightenin', I would!"

"Oh, Barney," says Osyth; "and see what you have done!"

"Niver a bit more than he did to me sister," retorts Barney. "But I'm sorry—yes, I'm sorry for it in me heart!"

"I don't know what to say to you, Barney," says Osyth; "you must come by-and-bye, and see mother. I'm very sorry about Teresa; come and tell us how she is to-morow."

And somebody else has another confession to make to-night. Me and grannie are alone in the drawing-room.

"I want to tell you about my badness, grannie," says Me humbly.

"Yes, come and tell me all about it Me, darling," says gentle grannie.

And penitent Me, with many tears, tells the story of the last few days—his selfishness, meanness, and unkindness, which have been the cause of all this suffering.

"My poor Me!" says grannie, when she has listened patiently to the end; "I've been blind to your faults, and I have not told you of them as I ought to have done. I am as much to be blamed as you. It was through my foolish love, Me, I did'nt mean to do you harm, I did not indeed!"

"Oh grannie!" exclaims Me; "when you've been ever so good to me always! And I've been"—the words will force themselves out—"an abominable pig. I wonder everybody does'nt hate me! I wonder the Mayhews are all so good to me! Grannie, if Baby dies, I shall have killed him!"

"God is very, very good to us, Me," says grannie, drying her own tears to comfort Me; "I don't think He will give you that great pain to bear all your life long. I don't think he means to take our darling from us. But, Oh, Me! let us both learn a grave lesson from this: I, to be clearer-sighted, and to show you your faults; and you, to pray and strive to amend them."

"I will, grannie, I will," says Me earnestly.

"Then, for a beginning—will you tell Cuthbert all you have told me?"

"Yes, grannie," answers Me bravely. "He ought to know. And I'll take it as a penance, grannie, that whenever I'm a pig, or mean, or cross, or any of my other badnesses, I'll go straight to whoever I've been bad to, and say I'm sorry; will that do?"

"God bless you Me," says grannie, laying her hands on the glossy brown curls of her darling, "and help you to keep your good resolution!"

"Now I'll go to Cuth.," says Me stedfastly; "it'll only get harder to do if I wait."

The next few days are a sad, sad time for the Mayhews, for their Christmas box—their Baby—is very, very ill. He has severe rheumatic fever, Dr. Milner says; and if he does not soon show signs of gaining strength, it will prove a hopeless case.

Mother watches Baby's cot night and day, as only mothers know how to watch; and prays for her darling, as only a mother can pray.

Baby is delirious with pain. He does not

F

know that she is there. He chatters wildly about the pool, the flowers, drowning Me, and the dreadful bear, until he screams with fright.

And every visit the doctor pays, he shakes his head, and looks graver.

"Oh, my Baby; my little Noel!" moans the poor mother, holding the little fevered hand in hers to cool it; "surely God will not take you from me yet—my Christmas child, who has never yet seen his father!"

But when she sees the poor little limbs all contorted with the dreadful pain, and she can do so little to soothe, she cries from her heart— "Oh my God, thy holy will be done!"

At last the crisis arrives, for which they are looking so anxiously, and Baby comes back to consciousness, very weak, and quite blind, to find mother sitting close beside him.

"He's not got nob'dy ense," are Baby's first faint words.

"Who, darling?" asks mother.

"God," says Baby, in his weak little voice; "he's not got nob'dy ense."

"Do you want to leave us, Baby?" says mother, with an aching heart.

"He's gwad, 'cos 'e pain hurts him so," answers Baby slowly. "He don' yike to yeave his mover, an' Car'l, an' e' yady. But mover would ten him to be kin'—an' God's got nob'dy ense!"

"God has all the glorious Angels and Saints, Baby," says mother sadly. "Don't you know?"

"Nob'dy ense. He wins' go," repeats Baby wearily.

The idea has taken such hold of him, that nothing can make him give it up. Mrs. Mayhew tells Dr. Milner when he comes next, of Baby's strange fancy.

"He is right. He is going fast, poor little lamb!" says the doctor. "I would not hide the truth from you. And there is this comfort if he recovered even he would be blind for life; see, here!"

And he shows mother the little eyes, terribly bloodshot, and almost closed.

"My little Noel!" murmurs mother, then. "God's will is best!"

"He's got nob'dy ense," whispers Baby dreamily.

Mrs Doran has driven up every day to inquire after Baby, and to bring him ice, and flowers,

F 2

and delicious fruits. She would like to help to nurse him, but Dr. Milner says the only hope for Baby's life is to be kept perfectly quiet. Only mother and Nanna may come into the sick room.

Barney Wheelan is another constant and affectionate inquirer after Baby.

One afternoon as he asks "How is the little masther to-day?" poor Barney bursts into tears, and quite shakes with his sobs.

"What is it, Barney?" asks Osyth, who answers the door herself now, so that there may be no banging to shake Baby in the room just above. "Baby is really a little bit better this afternoon."

"And it's glad to hear it I am!" says sobbing Barney. "But shure it's throubled sore I am for me little sisther that's gone in the night. And is'nt it meself that is left all alone in the cauld warld?"

"Poor, poor Barney!" says Osyth. "Was anyone with her when she died?"

"There was the praste an meself, miss," says Barney still sobbing; "an' the good Sisther that nursed her—may hiven's best blissin's be upon her, the angel! But they've taken Teresa away wid them. And its all alone I am wid meself. And I can't say a prayer were it iver so! And not a bite has intered my mouth this blessed day."

"Bridget, give Barney something to eat, please," says Osyth. "And there is sixpence for you, Barney. I'll go and tell mother."

Softly as Osyth speaks to mother at the door, Baby hears.

"Osif says yitten T'wesa is dead," he repeats; "mover is yitten T'wesa quite dead? Baby sink its weddy sad!"

"Yes, she is dead, darling," says mother. "Poor little Teresa! If she had lived, she never could have walked, and she would always have been deaf too."

"He's sinkin' which is 'e baddest," whispers Baby presently, "to be yame an' deaf, yike yitten T'wesa, or not to see mover an' anysing any, any more always?"

Then mother knows that Baby has heard the doctor say that if he lives he will always be blind.

"Whatever is God's will is best, darling," she answers sorrowfully.

"He sinks God's weddy kin', mover, to take poor yitten T'wesa," whispers the faint little voice again. "Yen God's got someb'dy ense now. Baby's weddy gwad!"

Then again—"Baby win stay wif mover, an' Car'l, an' awn of yem now, 'cos God's got someb'dy ense. He's weddy gwad!"

Mother hides her face and cries.

"Where's Car'l?" asks Baby presently. It is the first time that he has asked for any of the children.

"Car'l is in the schoolroom with the others. Would you like to see him when Dr. Milner has been, darling?" says mother.

"He *carn' see* Car'l," says Baby pitifully, "'cos he's not got no eyes yeft; but he would yike *to feen him*. Car'l can talk nice'y to 'e Baby."

Dr. Milner sees a wonderful change for the better in Baby. He seems much stronger. There is really room for hope now.

"God's got someb'dy ense," whispers Baby.

After the doctor's visit Caryl comes up, and, one by one, Baby sees all the children; even Me, who has to be brought into the room almost by main force by Cuthbert and Aloysius.

"I'm too bad to see him," he sobs. "He'll hate me. *Don't* let me go! If it hadn't been for me, little Teresa and——"

"Hush, Me!" says mother. "Be very quiet. It was God's will. Come in. Baby wants to see you."

Me comes fearfully forward to the cot, and Baby's little arms are soon wound round his neck.

"Was 'oo *weally* dwowned?" says Baby lovingly. "He twied to save 'oo out of 'e water, but he couldn't. An' mover's not got 'e nice yennow f'owers what Baby gaddered! P'or Me didn' get any martins' eggs, mover. Baby's weddy soddy! He win give Me *awn* 'e eggs what Cuff gaved him on 'e stwing in 'e nurs'wy. Don' kwy, Me! He carn' see 'oo, 'cos he's got no eyes; but he can hear 'oo's kwyin'."

"O, Baby!" sobs Me, "will you really forgive me—all about the bear, and everything?"

"'Oo's weddy soddy," says Baby, feeling Me's face with his soft little hand. "I sink 'oo's not goin' to be senfish any more."

"Now he would yike to have 'e yady," says Baby, when Me is gone.

"To-morrow, Baby, if you are better," promises mother.

And Baby is so much better next day that he is able to sit up on mother's lap, wrapped in blankets, with a bandage over his poor sightless eyes, when Mrs. Doran comes to see him.

"He carn see 'oo. It's awn 'e night," says Baby pitifully. "Put 'oo's face yow down, an' he can *feen* 'oo!"

And the little hands stray softly over her face.

"'Oo's kwyin'," he says at last. "Don' kwy. God's got someb'dy ense. 'E Baby's not goin' away!"

"But must he be always blind?" says Mrs. Doran aside to mother.

Mother nods her head. She is too sad to speak.

"Baby win get wenn," whispers Baby; "an' yen he win go an' have 'e nun's cwoss to make his p'or eyes better."

Baby has been repeating this over and over again all the morning. Mother thinks it is only a little sick child's fancy—Baby is very fanciful—but it clings to him.

"'E Nun's cwoss, 'e yitten Sister's cwoss," he repeats; "win make 'e Baby see nice'y."

"Try it; and trust Baby's faith," says Mrs. Doran.

So when he is well enough to go out, mother drives Baby to the Convent of the Little Sisters of the Poor.

"He wants to kiss 'e cwoss again," says Baby, when Sister Marguèrite comes in; "to make 'e Baby's eyes better."

"He asked so often for it," says mother, "that I felt I must bring him."

"Dear little one! Then, here it is!" and the kind sister presses it to his lips.

"He wants to keep it," says Baby, holding out his hands.

"My poor Baby has such strong faith that he will be cured of this terrible blindness by that crucifix," says mother.

"It has often been blessed in healing—this cross!" says the sister. "I venerate it. And remember, God does love to reward the faith of His little ones. Come now, and our old people shall say some 'Our Fathers' and 'Hail Marys' for him."

She leads Baby by the hand into a large cheerful room where the poor old men are gathered together. Some of them are working, some reading, some too old for either are nodding in their comfortable chairs. Whatever they are doing, they all stop when the visitors come in.

"I want you to say some 'Our Fathers' and 'Hail Marys' for this dear little one," says Sister Marguèrite. "See! He is left quite blind from a fever, but he has faith that the cross he is holding will cure him. When he is healed, we will say more prayers in thanksgiving."

"Ay, that we will!" say the old men, and very fervent prayers go up from those trembling lips, while Baby's weak little treble joins in.

"Now we will go and ask the prayers of our old women," says Sister Marguèrite. "We must have all the help we can get. Our prayers must be strong."

So the dear old women pray for Baby, too, as he is led into the midst of them by Sister Marguèrite, carrying his cross.

"Let us try to have the little child's faith," she says, as Mrs. Mayhew bids them good-bye, with tears in her eyes. "Our dear Lord will sooner work a miracle than disappoint one little one that believes in Him."

Next morning Baby's eyes are so much better that Dr. Milner is astonished.

"The doctor has done nothing," he says; "but the prayers are all-powerful. Pray on."

So mother and Baby visit the Little Sister's Convent again that day, and once more the good old people's prayers go up that the blind may receive sight. And Baby clasps the cross to him lovingly all the time. Even in his sleep, it has not been out of his tiny hand.

In a day or two the old people join with all the Mayhews in thanksgiving for a great mercy to the little child. The blind has received sight.

"He wishes could see 'e Jesus on 'e cwoss!" Baby had said wistfully; and when mother took away the bandage, the image of Our Loving Dying Lord was the first thing Baby's eyes rested on.

And I have both seen the cross, and heard the story.

CHAPTER IX.

CHRISTMAS AGAIN.

TIME flies on butterflies' wings, everybody knows, and certainly these happy midsummer holidays come only too quickly to an end for the little Mayhews.

Grannie and Me go home before the last days of the holidays; but it is no longer the same selfish Me, who forgot everybody else to look after the welfare of No. 1. Me has kept his good resolutions very faithfully on the whole, though they have cost him more at times than anyone but his Angel Guardian knows. For nobody grows good, or gets rid of even one bad habit all at once. Evil sticks to us like a leech. There must be many a fight—sometimes until death—and even many a bleeding wound before we are left victors in the field.

Ah, but it is well worth the struggle, well worth the pain—for the crown of heaven afterwards! What will it not be, then, to see Our dear Lord *satisfied* with us—to hear Him say that '*Well done!*' '*Well done!* that bad habit conquered there!—that step forward bravely taken; *well done!* This little sacrifice generously made for love of Me; *well done!*' And to see His Face smiling upon us; the smile of Our beautiful Mother; the happiness of our Guardian Angel; and the joy of all the Saints who have watched every step of our way with their love and prayers! Ah, it is well worth while—the struggle here!

But I must not forget that I am not writing a sermon—though to be sure they are grand things in their place—but a story.

Before grannie goes away, she gives Baby a real, new paint-box, with brushes, and saucers, and good moist colours, on condition that he does not suck the brushes, or put the paints into his mouth. Of course the young man's delight knows no bounds.

"Don't paint your frock, Baby, or the poor roses!" says grannie.

"He win paint a bootifu' picture for grannie," promises Baby; "Wif 'e mountings, an' 'e wivers, an' 'e twees, an' 'e mans, an' 'e womins, an' 'e houses, an' 'e twains, an' 'e cows, an' 'e woonfs!"

The result of Baby's efforts is a beautiful daub of bright colours, which lose themselves in one another with a grand general effect.

"Bless the boy!" says grannie, feeling in her "poppet" for some lozenges; "he has all his father's talent. Depend upon it, Magdalen, that lad will be an artist some day!"

"He win be a yartis'," echoes Baby.

Mother smiles. "These are early days for deciding what his profession is to be," she says; "though certainly that unfortunate 'b'oo flock' looked like a talent for daubing!"

When grannie has gone, poor Cuthbert's time for leaving home draws very near indeed. It is the first time that the boy has ever left home for longer than a fortnight or so, and he feels the parting very keenly. Mother and he indulge in many quiet talks all to themselves in her boudoir for several days beforehand, and the other children noticed that there are often tear-stains on his brown cheeks when he comes out. They don't make any remarks, however, for fear of hurting Cuth.'s feelings, which are very sore and tender just now.

Osyth and Magdalen dry their tears at the

thought of losing Cuth., to superintend the packing of a hamper of good things—" grub," Al. calls it, in his slangy fashion—for him to take with him, and they even manufacture some of the contents themselves with a little kindly help from cook.

To be sure, Magdalen does sweeten some of her cakes with salt, and flavour others deliciously with turpentine instead of essence, on one of her expeditions to the moon; as Cuth. and "the fellows" find out to their cost later on; and Cuth. says to himself—"That's Moonie to a T!"

Baby, too, is preparing a grand surprise for his big brother. For several days before Cuth.'s departure, he may be seen perched on the lowest bough of a pear-tree; his little legs dangling, his paper on his lap, and his nose nearly touching it, as he splashes away with one of those charming new brushes, and chatters to himself all the time.

The picture that he is painting is for Cuthbert, but Cuth. is not to know anything about it.

"'E twees is gween," says Baby thoughtfully. "He has'nt got any gween. B'oo would yook pwettier yan gween. He win paint yem b'oo."

"Yat's 'e twee on 'e yawn."

The hot little face turns up for a moment in search of a fresh idea.

"Yere's 'e pussen-cat on 'e yawn. Cuff would yike her to be dwawed."

"Yat's her tain."

"O dear! 'E cunours is awn yunnin' into 'e udders!" says Baby in dismay.

"'E sun is gwowing into 'e b'oo sky, an' makin' it gween!"

"Now he win paint 'e house wed, wif 'e chimbleys, an' 'e 'moke."

"'E house is awn tumbynin' down!" says Baby dismally, reviewing his work at arms' length; "an' 'muts's tain is yunning into 'e b'oo twee on 'e yawn! Baby sink it's weddy hard to dwaw a picture!"

A deep sigh.

"Now he win put 'e Baby, an' Cuff, an' Car'l, an' awn of yem into 'e picture," says Baby.

"Cuff's got a yong nose."

"Yere—Baby sinks yat's weddy yike Cuff!"

At last the picture is finished, and proud Baby carries it dripping in doors to be appreciated. Of course, everybody must see it except Cuth.

Mother admires it very much, especially smuts' fine tail, when she hears what it is.

Osyth begs for another picture like it for herself.

Moonie says it rather reminds her of Mr. Whistler's last picture in the Academy.

"Cuff can put it in 'e 'cademy, if he yikes," says the modest artist.

The twins want to have framed likenesses of all the toads.

Daisy and Bruno quite approve of the picture.

Cuthbert, Aloysius, and Caryl are sprawling over the schoolroom table, talking of last things. Cuth. must by no means see the picture.

Baby brings it round to Al., under his pinafore, keeping one eye on Cuth. all the while.

"He's been drawin' an' paintin' a picture for Cuff," he announces in a loud whisper. "Don' ten, Al.—it's a s'prise!"

"But what *is* it, Baby?" says Al.

"It's 'e house," explains Baby; "wif 'e yawn, an' 'e pussen-cats, an' awn of yem. Yat's Cuff."

"Bless us! What a nose!" exclaims Al. "You've made it as big as one of the windows. I'm sure Cuth. ought to feel flattered!"

"What is it?" inquires Caryl. "I say, let a fellow see young hopeful's performance! He, he! Ho, ho! Ha, ha! Well done, Baby! Excuse a fellow's smiling. It is'nt manners I know. But really this ought to be hung in the Academy —for all England to see!"

"Moonie said yat," says Baby with modest pride.

"Cuth's nose is worth anything!" says Caryl. "I really should like to show it to him; Baby, may I?"

"Esh," says Baby. "Cuff, Baby's been painting 'oo a bootifu' picture to go in 'e hamper. Cuff wins' forget *awn* about it, 'cos its to be a s'prise!"

"All right!" says Cuth. "Now, let's see. Is *that* meant for me?"

"Yat's 'Muts's tain," explains Baby. "Yis is 'oo, Cuff."

"Much obliged," grunts Cuth. "I should'nt have known myself."

"And you won't feel tempted to say with the poet—'O wad some power the giftie gee us, to see oursel's as others see us!' if *that's* how they see you, old fellow!" laughs Caryl.

"Now this ought to be Moonie," says Al., "with that great cloud on the top of her."

"'E paints did yem," says Baby.

"Well, I'm very much obliged, Baby, I'm sure," Cuth. says; "and we'll see about the Academy by-and-bye."

"Cuff wins forget awn about 'e picture," says Baby, carrying off his precious picture to be packed up; "'cos its a s'prise!"

"O Cuth.," groans Al., when Baby is gone. "What would'nt I give to be you! The girls have been busy messing in the kitchen, with their sleeves turned up, for the last I don't know how long. You will enjoy having such a lot of grub!"

"I would'nt trust Miss Moonie's pies one bit," says Cuth. "They'll turn out a queer compound of moonshine and green cheese, depend upon it. Never mind the grub, old fellow. Go in for your lessons like a brick after I'm gone, and when I've made a place warm for you at school, I want to get mother to send you up next term."

"And leave this poor wretch, like the last rose of summer, 'to mope on alone'!" says Caryl pouting. "All his lovely companions faded and gone. It's all very well for you, Master Cuthbert—but you've got your 'grub,' so be content, and leave me Al."

"Trust Al. to follow the grub, Caryl!" cries mischievous Daisy, coming in.

"Was there ever such a teaze!" says Al., pulling Daisy's goldie locks.

"Only one, and that's Al." says Bruno.

"An' yat's Al." echoes Baby following in the train.

Presently busy Osyth pops her head in, to say that Cuth's cab is at the door, and everything ready.

Then comes "good-bye," amid a hullabulloo of smiles and tears, and messages, and promises.

After Cuthbert's departure, the Mayhew world nestles under Miss Norton's wing in the school-room again. This term, Baby even joins the rest—proud of knowing nearly all his alphabet to begin with, and of being able to pick out his own name in a story-book whenever he meets it.

And so that little world wags on, with nothing really worth putting into print, until one November the Indian mail brings the news that father hopes to be home in about three weeks' time. The news spreads like wildfire in a moment.

"Hurrah! Hurrah! Hurrah!" cry Daisy and Bru.

"Ain't it awfully jolly?" says slangy Al.

"*Aren't* you glad?" the twins ask one another fifty times a day. Caryl goes about the house roaring "The Campbells are coming," at the top of his voice. If Nanna's head-piece were not uncommonly tough, it would certainly split. As it is she only smiles, and says—"Bless that boy! He's his father's very image."

"'E Tamins is tumin'," pipes shrill little Echo, following in Caryl's wake.

"Bless his little merry heart!" says old Nanna delighted. "Just hear him! Won't his father think him a bonny flower? And that it should be me that has the credit of him!"

Osyth, with Al.'s help, is making a big red and gold scroll, with "Welcome to Father" on it, to be nailed just inside the hall porch.

And Moonie has a dear scheme at heart to do father honour.

The children talk it over together, and Miss Norton has promised her help in carrying it out as grandly as possible.

Mother, of course, knows nothing about it.

"If we told mother our plans, we might just as well tell father himself at once, you know," Moonie says. "They can never keep secrets from each other."

"Shall you *really* be able to make it up out of your own head, Moonie?" says Daisy, filled with a sudden respect and awe for her big sister.

"Oh, no! Miss Norton will help me," says Magdalen humbly.

"But Moonie has written some dear little verses," says Osyth. "I've seen them. And this will please father so much, because we shall all be in it. It's such a capital way of showing Baby to him too."

"Moonie is what you call a poetess, I suppose," remarks Bruno thoughtfully.

"What's yat?" inquires Baby.

"Somebody who makes up verses, and all that sort of stuff," says Al. loftily. "I can't see much good in them myself. Old Virgil and Homer must have wasted an awful lot of time over theirs. If they had'nt, I should be saved the trouble of that 100 lines impot I have to write out for old Marsh to-day!"

"Sorry to hear you're in trouble, my friend,"

says Caryl, who is as happy in hot water, as out of it himself; " especially as it's with my old chum Virgil. Well, Magdalen, let's try over the first part of the affair to see how it goes. I suppose father 'll be here soon now."

But, as the old saying has it, "The best laid plans of mice and men gang oft a jee." There are rough winds, and storms at sea. Father's ship does not come in when it is due. Nor is there any letter or telegram from father. Mother gets anxious.

Cuthbert comes back for the Christmas holidays, full of tales of "the fellows," and still father is away.

Aunt Bee and her children, grannie and Me come to stay for Christmas. Everybody looks anxious about father.

"I do hope he'll come in time for Christmas day," says Moonie. And on Christmas eve there comes a letter to say that father has had a very long, stormy passage, but is safe in dear old England at last, and hopes to see them all soon after Mass on Christmas morning.

He's tumin' on 'e Baby's berfday!" cries four year old, delighted.

Early on Christmas morning, Mrs Doran drives

up with a beautiful basketful of hot house flowers to help in the children's surprise for father. Baby's "yady" is spending Christmas with them, of course.

"Se's not got nob'dy ense," as Baby says, and she is never so happy as when the little Mayhews are all round her.

Everything as regards the "plan" is in the pink of perfection when father arrives.

All the children, except Baby, and the grown-ups meet him in the porch.

"Where's my Baby — where's Noel?" asks father, as soon as he can find breath, after the hugs of the children.

"He's not visible yet, father," says Moonie mysteriously.

"They have got some grand surprise for you, Cuthbert," says mother; "but, of course, I'm not in the secret."

"Sit down a few minutes in the drawing-room, please, father, and talk to mother," commands Magdalen. "When we ring a bell, everybody is to come into the schoolroom, and sit down. The grandest chair is for father."

Then all the children run off.

Everybody laughs; but when the bell rings they all file off into the schoolroom like a lot of good, obedient pupils.

Once more, it isn't like itself—the dingy old place. It is gaily lit up. A carpeted stage is erected half across the room, and a great deal of whispering and giggling is going on behind the big crimson curtain that covers the bow-window.

Me Stanley, in gorgeous attire, and with a splendid pair of wings attached to his shoulders, a crown on his head, and a silver wand in his hand, comes forward; and motions father to sit down on a chair in the middle of the stage, adorned with pink paper roses.

Then Miss Norton at the piano plays the following lively little air:—

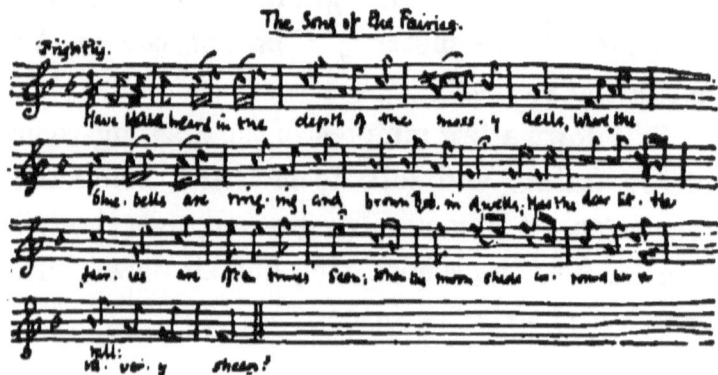

Me draws aside the crimson curtain, and forth come nineteen little fairies; the girls dressed in white and gold, the boys in blue and gold, with flower-wreaths on their heads, a coloured wand in one hand, and one of Mrs. Doran's beautiful flowers in the other. They form two pretty semicircles in front of father's chair, one within the other, and they all bow gracefully to him, with a grand flourish of wands.

Then the piano strikes up again, and all the children join in this little song of Moonie's own composition:—

"Do you know, in the depths of the mossy dells,
Where bluebells are ringing, and brown Robin dwells,
How the dear little fairies are oftentimes seen,
When the moon sheds around her a silvery sheen."

"Hey-day!" exclaims father; "but where's my Baby?'

Then the curtain shakes a little, and a little hushed peal of laughter comes from behind.

"Don't spoil the play, father; you must be patient," says mother.

Then the big children—I beg their pardon, fairies—of the outer semicircle advance a little towards father, and say—

"Ah, *we* are the little fairies bright,
And our hearts are warm, and our footsteps light!
We turn to a song
The whole day long;
Right merry and gay,
We dance away
The moonlit hours of night!"

"It's very Moonie!" murmurs father mischievously.

"Hush, father!" says mother. "There's a song now."

And all the children sing again:—

"Do you know, in the depths of the mossy dell,
How we heard in his song the brown Robin tell
It was coming, was coming this Christmas Day,
With someone we know, but whose name we wont say?"

"Very mysterious!" says father again. "But it's rather a cold time of the year for 'mossy dells,' isn't it?"

Then the little ones of the inner semicircle advance towards father's chair, and say:—

"Ah, *we* are the little fairies bright,
And our hearts are warm, and our footsteps light!
And *this* was the thought
The brown Robin brought—
Fairies of woodlands,
Wave your wands! [*Waving wands.*]

Bring a gift in your empty hands;
And come with your song so sweet and gay,
To greet him with joy on this Christmas Day."

Then the children of the outer semicircle say in turn:—

OSYTH.	From the valley I come.
MAGDALEN.	From my mountain home.
CECILY.	From the last sunbeam.
CUTHBERT.	From a crystal stream.
ALOYSIUS.	From the forest shade.
CARYL.	From a cool, green glade.
JUDITH.	From a silver cloud.
MONICA.	From the city's crowd.
WALTER.	On a swallow I fly.
HELEN.	From the rose do I hie.

Then the children of the inner semicircle follow suit.

KENNETH.	Fairy of the pansy.
EDITH.	Fairy of the tansy.
DAISY.	Fairy of the daisy.
NORA.	From the woodlands mazy.
WILFRID.	From the lily white.
BRUNO.	From the tulip bright.
AGNES.	From the foxglove's bell.
BRIDGET.	From a tiny shell.
PAT.	From the ocean strand.
ALL.	A merry band—
	We fly!
	We hie!

OUTER SEMICIRCLE. Whither?
INNER SEMICIRCLE. Hither!

Then the pretty little song breaks in as before :—

"What shall the fairies bring him, their love to tell?
How can they show him they all wish him well?
Come, fairies! Come, fairies! Say, what shall we bring?
We wave but our wands when we wish for a thing!"

"Couldn't be a better way of getting a thing you want," says father. "I think I'll ask the fairies to be good enough to bring me my Baby!"

"Oh, Cuth.!" says mother, "do be patient!"

Then the children of the outer semicircle ask, turn by turn :—

OSYTH.	A flower fair?
MAGDALEN.	A treasure rare?
CECILY.	Gold from the mine?
CUTHBERT.	A garment fine?
ALOYSIUS.	A sunbeam's ray?
CARYL.	A summer's day?
JUDITH.	Shall we bring him a sweet blue bell?
MONICA.	Shall we bring him the dear speedwell?
WALTER.	Shall we bring him the violet sweet?
HELEN.	Or the primrose at our feet?

Then the inner semicircle takes it up :—

KENNETH. Shall we rifle the store of the bumble
bee?
EDITH. Or bring him a pearl from the deep
blue sea?
DAISY. Or a nut from the squirrel's nest?
NORA. Or the fruit he likes the best?
WILFRID. Or the gift of a dewdrop fair?
BRUNO. Or a tress of golden hair?
AGNES. Or the clematis bunches hanging high?
BRIDGET. Or the painted wings of a butterfly?
PAT. Bring him a little of everything!
ALL. Fairies! Fairies! *What* shall we bring?

Now comes a very pretty little part of the play. The children of the outer semicircle move past father's chair, all of them presenting him with their flowers, bowing as they pass round to their places again, and repeating altogether:—

"We'll bring him flowers—he loves them so!
Fairest and sweetest of all that blow."

Then the little ones follow suit, repeating:—

"Ay, and the dearest songs we know,
That like crystal streams shall ripple and flow!"
ALL. "But better than all and everything,
The gift of a loving heart we'll bring!"

As they say the last words, Me Stanley throws back the curtain once more, and out comes dear Baby, got up in white muslin, roses, and wings—

a very cherub! He comes forward shyly to the children, who dance with him up to father, and leave him there; as they sing:—

"So father, our love and dear Baby's shall be
In warmest affection all given to thee.
And every good gift from our hearts we will pray,
May be given to thee on this Christmas day!"

Flourish of wands. The children are just going to vanish behind the curtain at once, when father, who has Baby on his lap, calls them back.

"And pray, who wrote this nice little play in Baby's honour and mine?" he says.

"Magdalen did," says Osyth with sisterly pride.

"But Miss Norton helped me a great deal," adds Moonie, blushing shyly.

"We ought to think ourselves well off," says father, "with an artist and a poetess in the family. And I suppose the twinnies will come under the head of naturalists, on account of those precious toads. Well, bravo, Magdalen! Bravo, my lassie! It was a very pretty little piece, and nicely acted to."

"It was a dear little play," says mother.

"But the end of it was quite the best part," says father, "for you gave me my Baby. God bless my little Noel! God bless all my bairns!"

"Amen!" mother answers softly, with shining eyes.

CHAPTER X.
FINISHING TOUCHES.

AND now my story, such as it is, is at an end; but as everybody has a spice of curiosity in their composition, and likes to know something more than the end—"the whole, and a thrifle more," as an Irishman would say—I am going to try to give you another peep at our dear Mayhew tribe many, many years later.

I don't think you would know father and mother Mayhew now if you were to see them, unless you were to recognise mother by the sweet smile that is so altogether hers. Their hair is grey, and you would not need spectacles to count the wrinkles on their foreheads and cheeks. Father is troubled with rheumatism, and mother manages somehow to creep about the house and garden leaning on her stick.

But their hearts are as young and warm as ever, for all that; and their old age is very happy in the sunshine of God's love, and with the love and goodness of all their children.

Grannie went home long, long ago—dear, sweet old grannie! People used to wonder that the angels left her so long on this earth when she was so ripe for heaven.

Me, her big, handsome soldier-laddie, was able to be with her to the last. She died with her gentle old hands resting in blessing on his head.

Osyth has been married some five years, and makes a capital little housekeeper. She has a tiny toddler of her own, called Magdalen, after grandmamma and the sister Magdalen, who has said goodbye to this world and its woes, and gone to be Our Lord's dear little nun in the Carmelite Order.

Strange to say, grandmamma Mayhew, who was always so wise and prudent with her own chicks, is doing her very best to spoil this little Maggie by too many lollypops, and by letting her have far too much of her own sweet way. And mother Osyth has to keep her eye on the two when they are together.

Cuthbert is a hard-working parish priest in a poor country mission. He is just the good, steady fellow that he always was, but the roughness and stubborness of his character has toned down into an honest strength of purpose, which he sorely needs in the trials and difficulties of his holy calling.

Aloysius is a barrister, still rather given to fits of laziness, but otherwise a very good fellow. He is married, and has a small son and heir, his own namesake.

Caryl has an appointment in the Indian Army, and means to follow in his father's footsteps on "the path of glory." He is just the merry, light-hearted fellow he always was, and a general favourite with everybody.

As to the twinnies—Kenneth is studying medicine, hoping to be a doctor some day, if his health will allow him. Edith is still a home-bird; but it is settled that when Kenneth gets some steady practice, she is to live with her twin, and keep house for him. They are as much devoted to each other as ever, and their being parted even for a time seems very hard to both.

Bruno has just passed his last examination for

the Indian Civil Service with flying colours, and is leaving England very soon.

And Daisy—little lowly, meadow flower of the flock—what of her? Ah, you know

"There is no flock however watched and tended,
But some dead lamb is there."

There is but one little green grave in the cemetery of the Mayhew name, and it is there they have laid her. Osyth brings little Magdalen every day to lay a fresh daisy-wreath on the grave of the auntie she has heard about, but never seen.

Next, and last, comes Baby, the hero of our little sketch. He is no longer Baby now, of course—big six foot high May-pole as he is!

Noel bids fair to fulfil grannie's prediction and become a great artist some day. Already his paintings have found their way into several first-class exhibitions; and his grand ambition—to have a picture well hung in the Academy—seems likely to be realised this year.

Fortunately for Noel Mayhew, he is not left, like most, a poor struggling artist, with only his pencil to earn his daily bread. His "yady," who died rather suddenly last winter—to the great grief of all the Mayhews, who had grown to love her dearly—has left all her property to Noel, so that he is really well off.

Noel has persuaded father and mother to let the old home, and to come and join him at Rosemount House.

So we will leave the Mayhews—good, and loving, and happy; happy, because they are loving and good.

Every Christmas tide all the members of the family do their best to meet together to share the Christmas joys, and to sing the joyful Christmas carols. Old Nanna is amongst them still; and in her easiest of easy chairs she delights to croon over memories of her "chicks," as she still calls them, though they have every one of them grown out of the "chick" stage long enough ago. And father and mother smile on their children, and chat together of that Christmas twenty-three years ago, when their Christmas gift came to them in the dearest guise of all—as a little, rosy, bonnie, blue-eyed BABY.

THE END.

www.ingramcontent.com/pod-product-compliance
Lightning Source LLC
Chambersburg PA
CBHW030249170426
43202CB00009B/681